She Wore Green

Larry G. Johnson

Vabella Publishing
P.O. Box 1052
Carrollton, Georgia 30112
www.vabella.com

This book is fiction. Similitude of its characters to any actual persons, whether alive or now deceased, is coincidental.

Cover art by Pam Ledgerwood. Pam was also the illustrator for *Little Orphan Andy,* and she did the cover art for *Walt's Mountain,* both by the author.

Manufactured in the United States of America

ISBN 978-1-957479-92-7

10 9 8 7 6 5 4 3 2 1

This book is dedicated to my friends who never let on if they thought I was losing my mind when I shared my ghost stories.

Part I: Two moments in time

Pearly White

"What do you know about the woman in green?"

"She's an off-duty nun in street clothes. The Sister was shot protecting her mother and needs to get to surgery immediately."

Pearl White had taken her elderly mother to her great-granddaughter's softball game. A gunman came up from behind the stands and started firing randomly. Three people were confirmed dead, and several more were wounded. When the shooter stopped to reload, he was subdued by the coaches.

"The Sister will have to take a number and get in line."

On the stretcher in the small-town hospital ER, the critically wounded woman came in and out of consciousness. She tried to speak and apologize for getting blood all over the sheets. Sister Pearl's mind kept going in directions that it had never been before and then revisited places where she once was.

In a moment of clarity, she asked about her family members and was assured they were okay. The trauma patient thought back over the events leading up to what happened. When she could get away, the nun enjoyed shedding her habitual garb. Her mother greeted her at the door and told her that her dirty blond hair looked good with her green outfit. The word dirty did not get past her.

Pearly White, as her youthful friends had called her, was a misnomer. And she knew it. A stain was forever woven into the fabric of her being.

"Am I dying?"

Sister Pearl's mindfulness was transported back to the time when she was taken to a home for unwed mothers. The spirit of the woman in critical condition was in anguish. No one heard her chilling words, and they brought no comfort.

"One time . . ."

"Only once in my entire life . . ."

"I had sexual relations with my sweetheart . . ."

"And I've been paying dearly for it ever since."

The popular teenager's first and only love was also completing his senior year in high school. He was already accepted at the state's prestigious university. She wanted to be a teacher. After they crossed the line, and the unintended happened, the young woman had no one to talk to. Fearing that her parents might disown her, she contemplated suicide.

In the mid-twentieth century, abortion was available only to those of means and with connections. Pearl's family had neither. Anyway, they were Catholic.

Not knowing where else to go, the girl in trouble turned to her priest. The Father worked behind the scenes to get her accepted into a residence for those in her condition. Functioning under the auspices of the church, the facility was also used as a recruiting tool to guide wayward young women to enter a convent. They were primed for a lifetime of devoted service, while endlessly seeking penance.

The midwife told Pearl how fortunate she was that a couple had agreed to adopt her baby. Her mind cleared enough to recall the conversation.

"Few folks want to take on another mouth to feed not of their kin. The Father had to put the fear of the Lord in them and heap on a load of guilt before they agreed. And girl, don't you go sniffing around trying to find your child. All records will be sealed. You need to pray every day that the little boy makes something out of himself even though he was conceived in sin."

Things were never the same with Pearl and her parents. They blamed themselves and each other for what happened on their watch. Most of all, they were guilt-ridden for signing over all rights to their grandson. If the Priest mentioned anything involving forgiveness, it did not take.

The pregnant girl came full term across town from where the baby's daddy was already enrolled in school. He would never know anything about this child.

The sperm donor's life was unfazed, but Pearl's was thrown into eternal disarray. Folks back home were told that she went to a boarding school, but her peers saw through the sham. After the baby was born, she meekly followed the lead of her superiors and became a nun. Some Sisters took on new names, but she kept hers.

The hospital patient roused when lifted from the stretcher to a bed. She heard voices but could not make out what they were saying. Sister Pearl's next awareness was a nurse leaning over telling her that she was out of surgery. The staff wanted to keep her awake, but the patient had no such inclination.

Fog shrouded her brain, yet the woman continuously extended her arms. Those attending presumed that she needed a hug. The delirious mother was instead reaching for her infant.

The nun's two families were told that she was in serious condition, and the next few hours were critical to her survival. Sister Pearl's vital signs were not encouraging.

A celestial light was dim at first. The dying woman focused her spiritual eyes on it as it grew brighter. The mortal's being was bathed in the peaceful luminance, and she felt clean. The glory beckoned her to keep going forward.

No longer bound by time or space, the mortal was ushered into the presence of Ultimate Being. Words were not spoken aloud, but telepathic communication flowed unobstructed. Before taking the final leap, the soul in transient had a request.

"Before I cross over, I want to see the child that came from my womb."

"This is a most unusual request but not unprecedented. I will arrange it. You will see without being seen. After your wish has been fulfilled, you may continue on your journey to the place prepared for you. Go in peace. I will come for you soon."

Mirror, mirror on the wall

Pearly Ghost's being was no longer restrained by the restrictions of her physical body. When she showed up inside a house, it never occurred to her to question where she was or how she got there. No one was home, so she went exploring.

"Look at you girl. You're walking on air."

Still adjusting to this new form of existence, the spirit looked in a mirror but could not see herself. It was as though she had always been like this.

The uninvited guest went from room to room without opening the doors. She could also move things if they were not too heavy. When she examined something, she tried to put it back just as she found it.

Dishes were in the sink and the mother wished to wash them and put them away. Might this spook her son? She saw no evidence that anyone lived with him.

The birth mother did not even know her boy's name. From mail on his desk, the poltergeist learned that it was Michael Jonas.

"Michael! My son was named after an archangel. And this Jonas did not come from the stomach of a whale. He came from my belly."

Waiting for the resident to return was effortless since time was irrelevant. As the shadows were getting long, she heard the garage door begin to open. The mother, who only got a glimpse of her baby before he was whisked away, positioned herself in front of the door that he was about to enter.

Would her son sense anything different? Might he feel her presence? The interloper heard the doorknob click and chuckled that she had no breath to hold.

There he was—A handsome middle-aged man. Mother Pearl tried to remember her son's biological father to see if there was a resemblance, but his face was a blur. She could not recall what she looked like, either.

The permanent resident turned on a lamp and booted up his computer. Pearly Ghost memorized the password. After checking the mail and news, he poured a glass of wine and took it to the deck. A gentle breeze stirred the wind chimes.

Mother Pearl was unable to take her eyes off the human figure that she gave birth to and then gave up for his own good. At least, that's what those involved wanted her to believe.

After Michael went to bed, Pearly Ghost hovered over him trying to connect with his soul. He was soon fast asleep oblivious to another presence within his walls.

Mission accomplished. Sister Pearl's request had been granted. She was now free to continue her voyage to the other side stretching out into all eternity.

A divine visitor

As if right on cue, Ultimate Being appeared. Once more communicating in ways unbeknownst to mortals, Sister Pearl was reminded that her entreaty was fulfilled. The Supreme Holiness reached to usher her across the Great Divide.

"Do I have to go so soon? There is so much more I want to learn about my son."

"I'm not sure that is wise. Too many things could go wrong."

"I promise that I will do nothing to alarm him. Since I did not get to raise my boy, can I just please enjoy him a little while longer?"

"Your request is granted, but if you violate your oath, you will have no further say-so in the matter."

How do you say giddy in ghoulish?

Much of Sister Pearl's earthly life was already fuzzy. She did recall discussions in the Sisterhood about the afterlife and even poltergeists. None of the nuns were even close to envisioning the purity of the light or the profoundness of the peace. What she had practiced as holiness was such a hollow shell. A skeptic when it came to spirits, she now was one.

Waiting for daylight, the supernatural part of Pearl White assessed her new existence. She had no brain, but she could think. Some things she could remember, but the vast majority of what was stored in her old memory bank was erased. The ghost was able to see and hear. When she spoke, nothing was audible to anyone else.

"Am I an apparition?"

The poltergeist conjured up a wraith-like human shape.

"Sister Pearl . . . You're no saint. No white robes for you."

Pearly Ghost selected mint green for the color of her garment, and straight to the mirror she went. Wow! She could see herself.

"That appearance will have to be put aside and only come out when it is safe. No need to frighten the wits out of anyone."

What a hoot

Michael got up and went to work. Mother Pearl had no idea what he did for a living and could hardly wait for her son to come home. She spent the time hanging around and adjusting to this new existence.

When he went out the door the next morning, the vehicle did not start up, and he was gone for almost an hour. The ghoul had not ventured outside the house and wondered where he went.

After lunch, Michael switched on the TV, and the shadowy house guest discovered a new toy. During an evening news broadcast, her son listened intently to a story about a nun saving her earthly mother's life during a mass shooting. The Sister's name was Pearl, and the convent had dubbed the main entry door, "The Pearly Gate," in her honor.

"Oh, my precious son . . . That is your mother they're talking about. How I wish you could know. 'The Pearly Gate.' What a hoot!"

Soon after Michael left for work on Monday, she turned the television on but found nothing of interest. For further amusement, she opened the filing cabinet where she found a folder containing Michael's report cards. From the signatures, she learned the names of her son's custodial parents. Mother Pearl had no way of knowing if he was ever told that he was adopted.

The mother also learned that her son was an excellent student, but his conduct grades were not always as good.

How does a ghost smile?

When Michael switched on the TV, he stepped back.
"I never watch that channel."

Pearly Ghost was paying attention. She must remember to always shut it down on the station that came up when she turned it on.

"Sister Pearl . . . You have so much to learn."

Pearly Ghost eavesdropped on a phone conversation. Someone was interested in buying her son's business. She had no idea what it was and learned nothing further over the next several days.

Meanwhile, the spirit savored the documents on the computer. Michael usually left it asleep, and she was meticulous not to change anything. She discovered his photo file and learned that he recently purchased a digital camera.

One afternoon, he came home early, and she scrambled to put the computer to bed. The desktop highlighted the last file opened. Mother Pearl did not have time to reopen and close the one underscored when she booted it up. Would Michael notice?

He came in, changed clothes, and went out the door. Pearly Ghost watched him head down the trail into the woods with his hiking stick. Quickly, she corrected her mistake and wondered if she could always cover her tracks.

The owner of a prosperous insurance agency had lots on his mind. He had received a firm offer to purchase his business. In his middle 50s, he was not sure what direction his life would take if he accepted it. Down on the creek bank with water cascading over a little fall, he made up his mind.

Self-unemployed

Spring was in Michael's step as he went back up the path.

"Michal Jonas . . . Soon, you will be 'self-unemployed.' It's high time for you to take back full ownership of your life."

When he came back inside, Mother Pearl saw the change in Michael's demeanor. She could hardly wait to find out what he had decided.

Pearly Ghost listened in as he placed a call, and she was very pleased that he was selling his agency. She would have so much more time to enjoy her son. Even so, her playtime might be limited to when he was out and about. There were always the nights when he was sleeping.

It took a few weeks for the transaction to be completed. Meanwhile, the spirit of Sister Pearl thought often of the beckoning magnificence awaiting her, but she kept postponing her return to be embraced by the light. The transient spirit also contemplated what humans call emotions. She was experiencing something undefinable. There was no reason to put a label on the purity of love.

No longer restrained by what people identify as time, Pearly Ghost, nonetheless, learned to follow a timetable. She figured out which days Michael went to work and the weekend when he was off. She also checked his calendar regularly to follow the countdown. Mother Pearl was so looking forward to having her little boy home around the clock.

The cutting edge

The day after Michael turned the keys over to the new proprietor, he embarked on his first self-unemployed project. Mother Pearl looked on. With only hand tools to work with, he began spading a little plot for an herb garden. Pounding with the mattock as though there was no tomorrow, the man free of a schedule got a grip.

"Slow down, chap. You've got the rest of your life."

Mother Pearl especially enjoyed handling the things that Michael often touched. She was careful to put them back as she found them but was sometimes careless. His pocketknife fascinated her. The apparition played with it while her son was preoccupied.

One night, she had a flashback of life in the convent. All Sisters had quirks. Hers was mischief. She delighted in hiding things from her elders and then letting them find the items in strange places. Sister Pearl recalled keeping a straight face when Mother Superior uttered to herself.

"I must be losing my mind."

Dare she? The ghost's old habits got the best of her. She removed the knife from its place with Michael's keys and pocket change and hid it where he would never find it.

Since he did not have to get dressed to go somewhere every day, it was several mornings later before Michael discovered that the knife was missing. Mother Pearl watched as he checked the pockets of the last trousers that he had worn. Not satisfied, he went through several other pairs of pants.

She followed him to the garage to see if it had fallen out of his pocket as he took his keys out. The man searched throughout the house, but the keepsake had simply vanished.

Michael feared the worst. The knife was a gift from his grandfather, and he cherished it as if it were a member of the family. He had carried it for years and could not imagine mishandling it.

Two days later, he reached for the pair of jeans that he wore the previous day, and the knife fell at his feet. It was positioned carefully on the hanger to fall with the slightest movement.

"So, there you are. You must have been in my watch pocket all the while and just now fell out."

Mother Pearl was ecstatic. She had pulled her first prank on her son. The ghost had brought her sense of humor along with her.

"Sister Pearl . . . That pocketknife feat puts you on the cutting edge of ghoulishness."

On purpose

Purpose was the catchword of the day. Michael renewed his library card, checked out a bestseller on the subject, and tried to make some sense of it all. His generation was discovering anew that life is purpose-driven. The middle-aged man was now thrust into a new phase of his earthly existence where it was time to reassess his own.

For several days, Michael processed his life situation. Was he fulfilling his purpose to the best of his ability? Not sure where the thought came from, he made a promise to himself that he would start keeping notes. That helped clarify things in his mind.

Mother Pearl looked on as he typed the first entries into the computer. From it, she learned things. The proceeds from the business deal were a tidy sum. The self-unemployed man had no aspirations for another career. Without indebtedness and with earnings from his investments, just maybe, he could get by without drawing a paycheck.

Gradually, the picture unfolded. Pearly Ghost looked on as Michael spelled out more things. Freedom was about to take on a new meaning. The man, with no binding obligations, was determined to view each day as a gift to celebrate and enjoy. It was his time, and he would make the most of it.

"No, Michael . . . It is our time."

The ghoul did a little inventory of her own. Sister Pearl decided that she had fulfilled two significant purposes. In very divergent moments in time, she brought a new life into the world, and she saved another from certain death. All else about her earthly life seemed irrelevant.

A helping hand

Mother Pearl ventured outside the house for the first time as she followed Michael on a walk through the woods. The specter was pleased by how at ease he was.

Michael stopped beside a little waterfall in the creek. His birth mother's spirit was working on how to read his thoughts. From his facial expression, he was at peace. She had also figured out that he addressed himself by his two given names or his initials.

"M J . . . That's not much of a waterfall, but when it's the only one you have, you're proud of it."

Michael talked to the birds, and they chattered back. A hawk was circling overhead, and Michael's lingo changed to a weird whistle. The red tail was thrilled to be noticed, and it responded with a series of squawks.

The hiker also used his camera to capture images of whatever intrigued him. Careful not to be an apparition, Pearly Ghost photo-bombed several shots. She was not altogether successful. When Michael uploaded the photos to his computer, he noticed some shadowing. He presumed the lens was dirty and cleaned it.

Michael was awakened out of deep sleep by a noise in the kitchen. The refrigerator made obtrusive sounds during the defrosting cycle, but this was something different.

Now wide awake, he lay very still. Was this a home invasion? Did he forget to lock the basement door? All was quiet, and after the adrenalin rush, he had trouble going back to sleep.

Pearly Ghost was playing with Michael's coffee mug when she dropped it. Fortunately, only the silence was shattered. She was still learning how to hold on to things.

"Sister Pearl . . . You are a spooky klutz."

It was time for Michael to rethink his security situation. Deadbolt locks were on the outside doors, and motion sensor floodlights covered much of the area surrounding the house. The most vulnerable spots for forced entry were the basement and garage windows.

Mother Pearl watched as Michael did some online research. After breakfast, he went to town and came home with decorative bars. The instructions were simple, but he ran into a problem steadying the restraints while setting the first screw. There was no way for him to know that he had a little help. His assistant also wanted to hand her son tools, but that was pushing it too far.

Got your back

The homeowner could now sleep sounder without worrying about a forced entry. While in the handyman mood, he took on another project. Mother Pearl looked on again while Michael surfed the web.

Both back doors to the home had glass panels, but the front entry was solid. He had intended to install a storm door since the house was built but never found the time. After doing his homework, he determined that he could make it happen by himself, even if the instructions said that it was a two-person job.

13

With dogged determination, he set out to prove the manufacturer wrong.

The glass-paneled door was more cumbersome than the window bars. Michael found out why the supplier recommended a crew of two as he struggled to hold it in place. Pearly Ghost stepped in once more with helping hands. The instructions were not wrong after all.

After the job was completed, Michael's only regret was not doing it sooner. Not only was more natural light welcomed into the lounge area, but he could now look out and see the deer when they were in the front yard.

The model he purchased also had a deadbolt lock. If someone came to the front entry, another layer of security was added. Relying on it, Michael did not always lock the main door.

When he opened up to let the light in one morning, he noticed something askew. The deadbolt was extended from the storm door, but it was outside its slot and resting against the frame, stopping the door from closing all the way.

Michael's analytical mind went to work. Perhaps, when he came inside last, the hydraulic ram had not fully released, and he switched the lock before the door was fully resting in place. He made a note to be more attentive.

A day or so later, he found the storm door in the same position. The perplexed man determined to check each time he went in and out to make sure it snapped into place before locking it. When he closed the main door for the night, he double-checked.

It happened a third time, and the man's mind went in search of improbabilities. The lock came with two keys. One was on his key ring and the other with the hidden house key. Only a select few knew where it was. It was unthinkable that somebody was slipping in and fixing the door like that just to mess with him, but just in case, he brought the keys inside.

Even with every precaution, he found the door ajar yet again. No matter how hard he tried, he just could not wrap his mind around any conceivable explanation.

Michael did a load of laundry, and a pair of bulky dark-blue woolen socks were in the wash. When sorting the clothes, one sock was missing. A quick check revealed that it was not left behind in the hamper, the washer, or the dryer. While he had heard others discuss disappearing socks, this was a first for him. Michael put the singleton in the drawer just in case its mate resurfaced.

Preparing for bed that night, he walked past the dresser in subdued light. His eyes were drawn to something on the floor. The missing sock was in his path. On other trips to the bathroom in broad daylight, it was not there. Hmm.

When he reached down for it and stood back up, something else in his line of vision was very much out of place. A pair of binoculars that he kept beside his chair in the den was atop the dresser.

Whoa! The binoculars often went with Michael to the deck, but he never had any reason to take them into the bedroom. He tried to imagine them in his hands when answering the call of nature. Might he have left them there on an urgent trip to the bathroom? He could not recall anything like that happening.

Michael was not sure where it came from when an inner voice whispered.

"Use your eyes."

Was that what the sock on the floor and the binoculars were telling him?

For some strange reason, he thought about the storm door. Everything was in working order, but Michael recalled when installing it that the deadbolt did not go very far into the hole drilled for it. He took the key and locked it from the outside. Then, he gave the handle a yank. Surprisingly, the door popped right open.

Michael realized that he was operating behind a false sense of security. The fix was simple. With spacers behind the catch to move it closer to the frame and longer screws, the storm door was now providing the protection that it was designed to.

Still, the man was unable to unravel the mysteries that moved him along. Neither did he yet grasp that an overshadowing entity was signaling something.

"My dear son . . . I've got your back."

Part II: Heaven can wait

What's going on here?

Little did the ghoul realize that a knotty situation was looming. Free to be, Michael was planning a road trip. Was she confined to the house? What would she do while he was away?

Ultimate Being was very much aware of Sister Pearl's predicament. The Supreme Being suggested again that it might be time for her to come along, but she protested.

"Time is irrelevant. I can wait until my son returns, but what I really want is to go along for the ride. Have I not proven that I can behave?"

"I cannot say that you have always received high marks, but you are trying. Go along, but just remember. You cannot stay in this state of suspension forever. And one more thing. Make sure Michael does not forget his pocketknife."

Pearly Ghost's mischief had not gone unnoticed, but she did not feel reprimanded. Neither did she realize that there was more to the instruction than just recognition of her prowess.

Mother Pearl watched as Michael got a suitcase down and put it back. Instead, he rounded up some crates. Socks and underwear went in one. Jeans and pullover shirts in others. An empty one was set aside for dirty clothes. Hanging garments went behind the driver so as not to block his vision. He would take a tote into a motel room with what he needed for the following day.

Deciding what to pack took some thought, and gradually, it all came together. Sorting travel stuff was no issue for Pearly Ghost.

The pilgrim decided to head out on Mother's Day. That weekend was always difficult to get through because he never felt any closeness with the mother who raised him. With a card in the mail, he wished to get ahead of summer vacationers.

The man's birth mother was thrilled with the departure date. It was always her worst weekend of the year. What better way to celebrate her day than by taking a road trip with her child? Michael had a hitchhiker who could not take her eyes off the one behind the wheel.

The second day was uneventful until Michael dozed off. Pearly Ghost jerked the wheel just before the vehicle ran off the road. With full attention restored, the driver thought a rut must have yanked the SUV.

"Whew! M J . . . Maybe you need to pull over for a little power nap."

Michael was meticulous with his belongings. Besides clothes, the only other things that he took into the room were a toiletry kit, his camera, and the computer. All had their places in the packing scheme. The camera rode up front, and the computer traveled on the passenger side backseat floorboard. His toiletries were tucked away in the cargo area.

When he went to brush his teeth one night, his toothbrush was missing. How could he have been so careless?

"Michael Jonas . . . If that's the biggest snafu, this trip will be a breeze. We'll stop somewhere tomorrow and pick up another one."

When the motorist went to hang up yesterday's shirt, his toothbrush was in clear sight on the floor behind his seat. How could that be?

His utility bag had not been near that area where it might have fallen out. On the road again, Michael reflected on the growing number of inexplicable things that he kept experiencing.

The storm door episode was especially puzzling. He might not be as sharp as he once was, but was he losing his grip? After all, dementia ran in his family.

"M J . . . What the heck is going on here?"

His alter ego had no answer.

A bystander

Michael kept a steady pace but stopped all along to take in the unfamiliar surroundings. They were largely wasted on Pearly Ghost. Although hovering just above the terrain of the world that she once lived in, the spirit now existed in another realm. In her former life, how she would have relished such a trip.

Perceiving the musings of her son's mind was stuck in low gear. The ghost paid close attention to his body language. There were always the takeaways when he brought M J into the picture or journaled his thoughts.

On the fourth day of the journey, the invisible passenger sensed that the driver was fatigued. Spontaneously, she began massaging his neck and shoulders—Gently at first so that her strokes were hardly detectable.

Gradually, the poltergeist applied more pressure. She was thrilled when he flexed his shoulder muscles. The spirit slowly backed off just as a rest area was coming up.

"Michael Jonas . . . I just had a wave of release come over my upper torso. Now, I need to stretch my legs."

Mother Pearl stayed behind when Michael went into the men's room. Even ghosts have modesty boundaries.

Back on the road, Michael switched off the radio and appeared to go deep into himself. Mother Pearl wished so much to go there, too, but for now, she was keeping an eye on what was up ahead. Sensing danger, she needed to get the driver's attention. But how?

The horn. But of course. One gentle tap and Michael refocused. The vehicle topped a hill where an accident had just happened. He slammed on the brakes just in time to avoid plowing right into an overturned pickup truck smack in the middle of the road.

A bystander suggested that he back up and turn on his emergency flashers at the hilltop to warn other motorists. Michael complied and then ran down to the scene. The truck had drifted to the shoulder of the road, the inexperienced operator oversteered, and it flipped over. The passenger managed to escape, but the driver was trapped.

Pearly Ghost watched as Michael smashed the window with a rock. He then took his pocketknife and cut the seatbelt. After removing dangerous shards, he pulled the young woman to safety. The accident victims were shaken, and they might well have internal injuries. Michael carefully moved them to safety away from the wrecked vehicle.

Another car stopped, but there was no cell phone service. The driver promised to go to the nearest house and call for help. Michael waited until the first responders arrived. Gas was leaking from the truck's tank. After hosing it down, an EMT thanked Michael for risking his life to save the others.

"That truck could have blown up at any moment."

"I'm just glad I came along when I did."

With sirens blaring, the accident victims were on their way to the hospital. Others had gathered, and Michael did not wait around until the law arrived. He was not an eyewitness to the accident, and they could sort it all out.

Mother Pearl, on the other hand, had a front-row seat watching her son in action. Her bias knew no bounds, and her admiration for Michael grew in leaps.

As he drove away, something hit him right between the running lights. Michael never saw the bystander again. And in the excitement, he had forgotten all about the horn toot.

Michael had trouble going to sleep that night. He prayed for the teenagers that they might make the most of their life reprieves. After he was finally snoring, Pearly Ghost caressed his pocketknife. Never again would she hide it from him.

Spending such quality time with her son was as close to Heaven as Mother Pearl would get in this suspended state. The everlasting was still ahead. She resisted the temptation to mess with him again throughout the remainder of the trip. Michael was adjusting to his new life apart from the rigors of the business world, and he did not need her distractions as his energies were rechanneling.

As they headed toward home, Michael was processing his experiences.

"Michael Jonas . . . We never know from one moment to the next just how much our lives hang in the balance."

His thoughts shifted.

"And a person is not qualified to use the word awesome unless he has seen the Grand Canyon."

Mother Pearl begged to disagree with the second part. Tagging along with her son was awesome.

After two weeks away, the vocal driver and mute passenger wheeled back into the yard. Pearly Ghost added "guardian angel" to her repertoire.

Visitors

The answering machine was blinking when Michael came in from washing the road grime off the SUV. Pearly Ghost heard the message when he pulled it up. His parents were on their way for a brief visit.

Michael was not a neatness freak, and he went into action. Soon, his residence was presentable enough. Mother Pearl wanted to help, but she constrained herself.

The folks didn't visit often and were barely in the door when Michael's mother mentioned that they were just passing through on the way home from one of her husband's business trips. She occasionally accompanied him.

Michael was not sure what was said next because his mind went straight to a nagging verity. His parents made sure, once again, that he was not a priority. Determined to be civil, as he always was, he asked about his younger brother and sister and their families. During the glowing reports, nobody could get a word in edgewise.

The only other topic of conversation was that Michael's father had finally decided to retire. He was already well into his 70s. Michael wondered how the couple might fare with so much togetherness. His mom could be overbearing. Nothing was said about his vacation. The cordial visit was soon over.

Mother Pearl did not know what to think about the two people who raised her son. Wasn't she supposed to be grateful for all they did for him when she was unable to? The spirit of the birth mother was glad that they did not live close by.

"Dear God . . . If that's wrong of me, please forgive me."

She was not the only one sorting things out.

"Michael Jonas . . . Why do my parents gush over their other offspring and treat me like a redheaded stepchild? And something else. Did you think Mother was a bit hesitant in some of her speech? I've never known her to stutter."

When Michael journaled the incident, he mentioned what a struggle it was to disallow negative thinking. Putting the exclamation point on his perspective, he spoke again with no clue that anyone else was listening.

"I'm so glad that God never takes time off and puts me in charge."

Mother Pearl wondered if her son could feel her surreal arms around him.

Part III: A moment of truth

Busted

Michael was unhappy with the location of the wall clock. He recalled the first evening after he moved into the new house. Sitting in almost pure silence, the only sound was the ticking of the antique timepiece. Chiming the hour and half hour, it was like the heartbeat of his home.

The dweller could not see the face from his favorite chair and decided that a better location was on the other side of the room. The clock was heavy enough that the homeowner wished it well anchored. Mother Pearl stood by as Michael mounted the step stool and ran a stud finder along the wall. It performed its magic, and a nail went right through the drywall into the solid wood.

Pearly Ghost was taking it all in. A tall bookcase was adjacent, and the handyman put his tools atop it while he was working. After the clock was moved, Michael stood back admiring his work. He was pleased.

Later that day, something started niggling in the back of his mind. He remembered putting the stool in its place beside the refrigerator and the hammer and nails back where they belonged. But not the stud finder. He ran his hand along the top of the oversized bookcase to retrieve it but could not detect anything.

Did he put it away absentmindedly? A quick check revealed that it was not in the drawer where he kept it. Just to be sure, Michael got the step stool back out so that he could see the top of the bookcase. He then retraced his steps to make sure that he had not inadvertently laid it down somewhere. No stud finder.

"M J . . . How could that tool just vanish into thin air?"

Later that week, Mother Pearl noticed that Michael was dressed to go somewhere. She thought about tagging along but preferred having her son all to herself. If she had gone with him, she would have been privy to some interesting conversation.

Michael was having lunch with two old friends. While chatting, he mentioned the inexplicable happenings that he was experiencing. Without batting an eye, one longtime acquaintance spoke with an air of confidence.

"Michael . . . You have a ghost."

"I wondered about that, but I have a hard time letting my mind go there."

The other woman weighed in.

"Don't I remember you saying that there was a ghost in the office building where your agency was?"

"Yes. The previous owner informed me that the place was haunted. The same was said of several other old buildings in town, but I was unimpressed. It did not take long for me to rethink my ambivalence. My employees routinely reported that files were rearranged during the night and stuff moved around in the kitchen."

"Did you ever see the ghost?"

"No, I didn't. A bit cavalier, I dubbed the mischief-maker, Billy Ghost. Someone who claimed to have seen the apparition told me later that it was a female. Thereafter, she was called Billie Ghost. Billie got blamed for anything awry whether she had anything to do with it or not."

Still trying to find footing, Michael mentioned that he took a college course in parapsychology and had an open mind about the paranormal. The discussion lulled as the diners returned their attention to lunch. Then, Michael asked a compelling question.

"Has Billie Ghost followed me home?"

"No . . . That spirit has nothing to do with you and is confined to its location. This ghost is part of your history."

"Could it be tied to the geography that I just happened to build a house on?"

"I cannot say for sure, but I don't think so. If that were the case, you might well be treated as an unwelcome intruder. You have a friendly ghost."

"For the life of me, I cannot imagine who it is."

"Back to your missing device, here's what you need to do. Go home and stand in front of the bookcase. Then say aloud something like this."

"Whenever you are finished playing with my stud finder, would you please put it back? I don't use it often, but when I do, it performs an important task."

"I'd feel like a fool doing such a thing."

"Your call, but if you want to know, for sure, what's going on, this is the best way to find out."

While Michael was away, Pearly Ghost toyed with the stud finder. She loved squeezing it and watching the red lights blink. Maybe she should place it back where she found it. Or, perhaps put it where it belonged. The impish spirit discounted that option. It might be months before he discovered it. For now, she decided to hold onto her plaything.

By the time Michael returned home, the friend's recommendation was not front and center. It stayed buried for a couple of days until he reached for a book. Again, he ran his hand along to the top of the bookcase just in case.

"Michael Jonas . . . You are about to witness one of the most ridiculous things that I have ever done in my entire life. And there have been some doozies."

With that, he blurted out the formula. His lunch friend had not indicated how long it would be before he might expect results.

Pearly Ghost was panic-stricken. He addressed the words to her as though he knew she was listening. The ghost was terrified. Was she busted? Might Ultimate Being think she had overplayed her hand and overstayed her welcome? The troubled spirit feared the worst.

This highly significant development did not get past Sister Pearl's Superior. The Creator approached the creature suggesting again that the time had come.

"Oh, please. I cannot go without saying goodbye."

"That might be problematic under any circumstances."

"Oh, please. I'll do better. I promise."

"I will once more grant your request, but only because Michael can use some excitement in his life. You must be more careful. If you had returned the mechanism earlier, this would not have happened. I'm putting you on probation. Should Michael figure out that a spirit lives with him as he now suspects, he must not know that it is his birth mother. He was never told that he was adopted. While his custodial parents had their shortcomings, they were honorable for taking him in. We must do nothing to hurt any of them."

The Almighty offered no advice about what to do next. Should she keep the stud finder hidden? If she put it back, Michael would have every reason to suspect that he had a poltergeist. On probation, Pearly Ghost agonized over what to do.

When Michael looked up at the clock, he glanced over at the bookcase, yet again. Finally, his curiosity got the best of him. Feeling just as nonsensical as he did when he said the prescribed words, he reached up.

Chills ran up and down his spine. Not for a nanosecond did he have any doubt about the device being there all along. Was it true? Did he have a ghost?

The next day, Michael took a full sheet of paper and wrote two questions.

"Who are you?"

"What is your name?"

He left it on a table in plain sight with a pen beside it.

Every energy particle that made up Mother Pearl's spiritual being wanted to pick up that pen and write in bold print.

"Pearl."

"Your mother."

Already on probation, that would undoubtedly terminate her time with her son.

The ghoul was stymied. Was she now relegated to being a bystander? That went against her nature, but she could not risk crossing the established boundaries.

Michael remained calm, but his senses stayed on high alert. He was disappointed that his overture went unanswered. None of the happenings made him fearful. Whatever this entity was, he did not feel unsafe. Pearly Ghost decided to cool it. During the next several weeks, there were lots of observations but no new manifestations.

Best wishes

Mother Pearl listened in on a phone conversation. She had no idea who Michael was talking to, but she picked up on something. His birthday was the following day. It was the anniversary of when she gave birth to her son.

Pearly Ghost scratched her spectral noggin for several hours trying to come up with some way to commemorate the occasion. Still sorting through the extent of her powers, she was unable to come up with anything. While he was sleeping, a possibility materialized.

Michael stumbled out of bed the next morning singing loudly.

"Happy birthday to me."

"Happy birthday to me."

Mother Pearl looked on with anticipation as he fired up the coffee maker for an early caffeine fix. She grew more impatient as he checked the TV morning news. And then, her wraith-like feathers drooped as he got dressed to take himself out to breakfast. Her baby boy's surprise was waiting when he returned.

While in town, Michael bought groceries. Included was a ribeye to throw on the grill later in the day and wine to sip while it was cooking. Eventually, he returned home.

After putting the groceries away, the moment Mother Pearl was waiting for finally arrived. Michael took a seat and woke up his computer. Instead of the scene that normally greeted him, the words, "Happy Birthday" appeared in big bold green letters.

The birthday boy was taken aback. How did the computer know that it was his birthday? Had he been hacked? Would touching any key unleash a malicious virus?

Michael's birth mother did not anticipate the consequences of her gesture. She stood by as he placed a call to the geek at the computer store. The phone was on speaker so she could hear both sides of the conversation.

"Is your virus protection up to date?"

"Yes."

"Do you store personal information on your computer?"

"No. Nothing personal goes on my hard drive. It's all stored on a CD. Do you think it might be infected with a bug? I purchased it at your store."

"That's highly unlikely, but let's check to be sure. Get it and insert it in the disc drive."

Michael complied and followed instructions to run it through a virus scan. Nothing was found.

"Open a browser and let's see what happens."

It came up without incident.

"Open other programs."

They booted right up.

"Have you ever received an e-birthday card?"

"Not that I can remember."

"Weird things happen with electronics. We may never know what this is about. Call me again if you need any further help."

"Thank you."

The greeting was gone the next day. Mother Pearl was bemused by the bedlam she had caused but very disappointed that she received no credit for the best wishes. Nevertheless, a tradition was established. If she was still around come his next birthday, Michael would receive another computer greeting.

Oops

Michael was spending an usual amount of time on the phone. He was also away more than common. Pearly Ghost suspected that a woman might be involved, and her suspicions were confirmed when a female was with him when he came home one day.

Mother Pearl had an instant dislike for her son's new lady friend. She knew he was lonely, but he could do so much better. Still, she felt powerless to do anything about it.

The witch showed up unannounced one evening with a bottle of wine and a decorative plate adorned with various kinds of cheese. Michael was perturbed that she did not call ahead, but he did not wish to be unkind or appear ungrateful.

The invisible spirit felt like she should give the couple some privacy, but her curiosity prevailed. Her son just couldn't let it go. This breach of his space was the tipping point. Maybe he should have realized that his uninvited date drank more than he did, and this was not a good time to discuss anything. Ready to move on, he forced the issue anyway.

The woman became belligerent. Michael had to restrain her from breaking things before pushing her out the door. Mother Pearl cheered.

In his haste, Michael forgot about the fancy plate. He wished for no further contact with the woman and did not know how to return it.

Pearly Ghost knew what to do, and she waited for her chance. After Michael washed and dried the plate, he sat it down close to the edge of the counter. With his back turned, she gave it a nudge. When it hit the floor, all the king's horses and all the king's men could not put it back together again.

"Huh, you old hussy. I can break things, too. That souvenir will not be around to remind my son of you."

Michael thought his carelessness caused the crash and did not mind at all cleaning up the mess. There was something therapeutic about it.

"M J . . . It will take a very special woman to replace none."

Christmas presents

The end of the year festivities were fast approaching, but Michael was showing little enthusiasm. Mother Pearl kept searching for a way to give him a present, but that was tricky. He did only a small amount of decorating, which included a candle in a dinner table centerpiece.

Pearly Ghost put on her Christmas green, but she stayed out of sight. When her son came in from a brisk winter walk, the candle was burning.

"So . . . You *are* still around. I've missed you. Hello to the ghost of Christmas *present*."

Angels sang on high, and joy filled Pearly Ghost's spectral world. Her son had just given her the best Christmas *present* ever. Michael missed his mama. He just told her so.

Clockwork

Michael was pleased with the relocation of the old wall clock. He could see it from his special chair and the sofa. It was older than he was, and the springs were not as strong as they once were. The eight-day clock needed winding every seven to keep it running. That became a Sunday ritual.

The clock kept good time until it was almost run down. Michael glanced up at it going out the door for a meditative Sunday walk and noticed that it was almost ten minutes slow. He made a mental note to wind and reset it when he returned.

As the man of the house reentered the living room, he stopped abruptly. The clock was no longer ticking, and the door was ajar.

"Wait a minute, M J. I didn't do that. I'm certain I didn't."

If a hand covered a winding stem, Michael sometimes opened the door to let it move past. The clock had stopped at straight up 10:00 with both stems in plain sight. A big smile showed up on his face.

"Whoever you are and whatever your name is, thanks for the reminder."

Michael was not the only one who smiled.

Part IV: Turning the page(s)

A new leaf

The calendar had no significance for Pearly Ghost in her deferred state. Starting a new year meant only a little more to Michael. He was out from under the burden of closing the books and preparing his business taxes. Still, he was raised during an era when New Year's resolutions were a part of the culture.

The self-unemployed man decided it was time to do a little soul-searching. The once prominent civic leader was now mostly a recluse. Associates could not understand why an able-bodied man did not get up and go to work each day.

The proceeds from his investments were keeping him afloat. In his personal inventory, Michael determined there was no one that he needed to impress. He was not dependent upon anyone's approval and relished getting out of bed most mornings with no set agenda.

Mother Pearl might not have known what her son was thinking except for his journaling. Prompting him to record his thoughts was one of her greatest accomplishments thus far.

Michael had given up on self-improvement. He was who he was. The computer novice was connected to the world wide web, and its usefulness was improving exponentially. He routinely surfed when researching something.

The man's thirst for knowledge was not quenched. He went to his favorite bookstore and brought home several field guides. Learning to identify the flora and fauna within his domain was a big part of his new resolve.

Michael kept trying to put his finger on something else that was calling him, and he finally figured out what it was.

Experiencing manifestations of a spirit dwelling alongside him, the mortal wished to learn more about the supernatural. He went to the library, checked out several volumes that addressed the paranormal, and he immersed himself.

Mother Pearl was curious when he came in with an armload of books and often read right along with him. She was delighted that her son wished to know more about her world. The ghost was also bemused by the ignorance and misconceptions of some so-called experts.

Certain information seemed to confirm what his friend had told him earlier. Some ghosts are situational, and for whatever reason, confined to a locale where something traumatic happened. Billie Ghost was like that.

Michael built his house a couple of hundred yards down in the woods where no other structure had ever been. Could this be a Native American spirit? He thought that highly unlikely because such a ghost would have no interest in his personal life.

Some writers suggested that other poltergeists are relational and usually quite benign. Michael particularly enjoyed a book written by a woman who claimed that her friendly ghost was that of a son who died when a child. His antics were similar to the ones he was experiencing.

"Michael Jonas . . . You've had no such loss. Wish we could figure out whose spirit this is."

Mother Pearl longed for a way to reveal her identity without being the instigator. Even so, that could jeopardize her stay with him. For now, she would continue biding her time, enjoying her son, and playing with him all along.

A call from home

Michael was surprised when his dad called. After some meaningless chitchat, his father asked if his son had noticed anything different about his mother. Michael remembered that her speech was a little slow when they visited, but he waited to see where the conversation was going.

"She was diagnosed with Alzheimer's sometime back, and it is progressing."

"Can anything be done?"

"Some clinical trials are promising, but nothing is on the market yet."

"Is there anything I can do?"

"Michael . . . I know that you are not a practicing Catholic, but will you please pray for her? And me, too?"

Not sure that his prayers might be of much value, Michael agreed.

"Are you managing without outside help?"

"So far."

"I can come and give you some relief if you need me."

"I don't think that will be necessary."

Left unsaid was the concern that in his wife's fog, she might say something about her oldest child's parentage. All of the nagging doubts regarding whether Michael should have been told years earlier resurfaced. Not sure how their son would handle being deceived was the tipping point to stay the course.

"M J . . . I wonder why he waited so long before telling me this. Then again, I'm always the last to know anything."

Soup's on

Michael ambled into the kitchen rubbing his eyes after coming out of a deep sleep. As his vision cleared, they were drawn to a strange phenomenon. He almost stepped in some water on the floor. This was no ordinary puddle. Rather, the liquid was in the shape of a perfect circle.

"Michael Jonas . . . What the heck is this about? What could have possibly put the water in that configuration? I couldn't duplicate that if I had to."

Michael decided to leave it be while he was figuring out what going on. He peered down at the anomaly several times more perplexed than ever.

Preparing lunch, the bewilderment found some footing. The night before, Michael had moved a jar of soup from the freezer to the refrigerator to let it begin thawing. Fully expecting it to still be partially frozen, he was surprised when it was fully thawed.

Then, it hit him. The ring of water was the precise size and shape of the jar. He held it over the water circle to make sure, and it was a perfect fit. His friendly poltergeist had taken the soup out of the fridge during the night and put it on the floor. Condensation ran down the vessel and formed a circle.

"So . . . It was you. Thanks for getting my soup ready."

Pearly Ghost was delighted that she got the credit. However, after all of his research and pondering, Michael was still no closer to resolving the mystery of his invisible housemate's identity.

"M J . . . This is about the best soup that I've ever tasted. At least, she didn't poison me. Did I just say, *she*?"

The bookworm

When Michael returned the books to the library, he looked for something else to read and selected a mystery. He was never addicted to television. After catching up on the news, he settled into his favorite chair on a cold winter night. In the lamplight, he read himself to sleep.

He picked up the book a night or so later and realized that he had not pegged where he got to. Before finding his place, he went looking for a bookmark.

Pearly Ghost was paying attention. When he closed the book, she waited until he was fast asleep. Then, she moved the marker.

Mother Pearl could hardly wait until her son's next reading session. She observed his confusion when he did not recognize where he left off. After doing some scrambling, he started reading but not before addressing his sidekick.

"M J . . . Were you sleepwalking when you put the book down?"

Disappointed that she did not get the recognition she deserved, the spirit went into action again. This time, she removed the bookmark and placed it under the book.

In so doing, Pearly Ghost added a new entry into her playbook. She had already figured out that Michael went searching for a rational explanation for anything outside the commonplace. Thereafter, if there was doubt in his mind about her being involved, she followed up with another ploy.

Michael still did not catch on. When the marker was not in the book, he presumed that he closed it absentmindedly and vowed to be more attentive.

Pearly Ghost was not about to let it go at that. After the next time Michael finished reading for the night, she put the bookmark back in the desk drawer. This was so much fun.

A big smile took over Michael's face when he next picked up the book.

"You again. Congratulations, you really had me going this time."

With smug satisfaction, Mother Pearl watched her son read. She was worming her way more and more into the bookworm's heart.

Picture this

As Old Man Winter began losing his grip, Michael was happy to be outside more. Digital cameras were much improved. The prices had come down significantly, and he purchased a new one that was pocket-sized.

The amateur cameraman's new endeavor was to build a photo library of the wildflowers that grew in his domain. This was an ongoing project because they blossomed at different intervals from spring through fall.

When he went out the door for walks along the trails on his property, a field guide was in his hip pocket, and the camera was in a front one. The wanderer was not single-focused. He also snapped shots of other things that reached out and grabbed his attention.

Rather than ditch his first-generation digital camera, Michael put it in the console of his vehicle. It was readily available should some marvel wishing to be captured avail itself while out and about.

Retrieving it one day, it would not boot up. He presumed the batteries were dead and reached for extras that he also kept handy. When he opened the compartment, the old ones had been removed.

After reloading and capturing the image, he did a little mental inventory. He recalled the advice about not leaving batteries in devices for extended periods when they are not used regularly. Had he taken them out as a precaution and just forgotten?

When finished with the camera, Michael made the conscious decision not to remove the power cells. Should he need it quickly, he determined that the risk of a leaky battery was not that great.

Pearly Ghost was disappointed that Michael did not associate her with the caper. The next time he reached for the camera, it again refused to come to life. The batteries were once more removed, but this time the compartment door was left dangling. He got it that time.

Michael was surprised when he received an invitation to a Thanksgiving dinner hosted by his sister. No matter how hard he tried to be a big brother when they were growing up, he was never close to his siblings. Mother Pearl decided to go along, but she promised herself that she would behave.

The family matriarch apologized for not being able to host the event. Ten minutes later, she repeated the same words. Both times, family members reassured her that it was okay. The expression of regret was repeated several more times as though for the first.

Michael pulled his dad off to the side. The man confirmed what was becoming apparent. The brain disease was progressing steadily.

As the family was seated around the table, the patriarch proposed a toast. He went to the kitchen drawer to retrieve the corkscrew. The man went scrambling. This was nothing new. His wife was always misplacing things.

When he returned to the dining room with an apology of his own, he glanced down and the opener was beside the wine bottle. Michael smiled, but no one saw him.

As the oldest son was saying his goodbyes, he waited to speak to his mother last. She looked up puzzled.

"Who did you say you are?"

"I'm Michael, your oldest son."

"Oh."

His dad stepped in.

"Michael has to go now. Say goodbye to him."

Michael took his camera but left it in his coat pocket. Others were taking photos, and he did not wish to be intrusive.

He set out the next day to get a good shot of a Christmas fern to use as the computer backdrop during the season. When he inserted the camera card, another photo was also uploaded. It was taken as he was saying goodbye to his custodial mother.

"Michael Jonas . . . Somebody must have noticed that I was not taking any pictures, found my camera, and took this to surprise me."

Pearly Ghost never ate a bite of food nor a sip to drink at the Thanksgiving gathering, but her wraith heart was, nevertheless, filled with cherubic gratitude. She knew who that somebody was.

Michael got no Christmas invitation from any family members. He called and spoke with his dad about a short visit, but the man dissuaded him from making the hour's drive. Unspoken was his father's concern. When his wife asked who Michael was as he was leaving after the Thanksgiving visit, he held his breath. The husband was fearful that she might blurt out, "You're Michael, my adopted son."

Preparing to celebrate alone, well almost alone, he decided to bring out a nativity scene that he had used in his office window. His favorite cloth to place the figures on was a silky, burgundy tapestry that faded some during the years adding to its appeal. The fabric had a flair of royalty about it and contrasted well with the decorative pieces. When he went to the dresser where he stored accent piece goods, it was not where it belonged.

By no means an obsessive-compulsive person, Michael generally followed the old admonition from his youth of a place for everything and everything in its place. There was no other location where he might have stored the cloth. Even so, he went through the closets and other drawers, and he could not find the regal-like material.

A Christmas green tapestry atop the pile was selected as a substitute. After the season was over, and he dismantled the nativity set, the shiny reddish cloth was back in the drawer right where it was supposed to be. Pearly Ghost was partial to green.

Things that go bump

The spirit presumed that she was not incurring Divine disfavor. Ultimate Being had not checked on her for quite a while.

Days were spent tracking her son's activities and nights amusing herself. She still had not conquered clumsiness and often dropped things. The ghost enjoyed rearranging stuff and then putting it back like it was. She was not always able to detect how much disturbance she was making.

Michael slept through most noises, but he was occasionally awakened when things went bump in the night. Immediately startled, those episodes were no longer disconcerting.

Otherwise, days and sometimes weeks passed with no detectable otherworldly activity. Michael gave his invisible guest little thought until something out of the ordinary got his attention. He had a good laugh when he blamed something on her but then found a logical explanation.

Pearly Ghost had a penchant for sharp things and often played with the kitchen knives. One white-handled paring knife especially fascinated her. She decided to hide it and see how long it would take for Michael to find it.

When he reached for the cutting tool and it was not in the holder, he did a quick assessment. That knife never left the kitchen. He checked and it was not in the dishwasher. Did he absentmindedly put it in a drawer? Mother Pearl looked on utterly amused.

After a thorough search, the knife was not located. One place he did not think to look was on top of the trash in the can under the sink. She put the knife there thinking Michael would discover it the next time he put something in.

It just so happened that it was time to take the garbage to the convenience center. He grabbed the trash bag and pulled the drawstrings. The ghost watched in dismay as it went out the door and into the vehicle. The recyclables were already loaded. It was too late to retrieve a favorite toy.

Michael kept waiting for the paring knife to show up somewhere. He even appealed to his ghost to return it, but its slot in the knife caddy remained empty.

Pearly Ghost learned a lesson. Some spots are not good places for hiding things.

Michael's digital wildflower file was growing. He also became fascinated with mushrooms but did not trust his expertise to determine if any were edible. On most adventures into the woods, he remembered to take his camera. If he forgot, it was just as well. These were times when his mind did some wandering of its own.

Mother Pearl was always taking things in. When Michael came in from one outing, he opened the camera to upload photos of the lush ferns along the creek bank. The memory card was missing.

The first place to look was the computer slot, and that's where he found it. Presuming that he was preoccupied the last time he used the camera, he put it back in and retraced his steps. It did not occur to him that he typically left the camera compartment open until he reinserted the card.

"Well, Michael Jonas . . . You got in some good exercise today."

Pearly Ghost was disappointed that she received no acknowledgment for the wily maneuver. The next time Michael was about out the door, his camera was missing. After a brief search, he took the old one in his SUV. His mind kept returning to places where he might have left it.

When Michael came back into the house, the pocket camera was in its usual parking place on the little table beside the door.

"So, it was you. Good one. You fooled me big time."

Remote possibilities

Michael was not much of a creature of habit. Yet, some routines were inevitable. He usually turned on the TV while sipping his first coffee to check on the morning news. One September morning, he slept late and almost missed it.

Now ready for a late breakfast, he switched off the television. As he turned to walk away, it came back on. He repeated the process, and it sprang to life once more.

"M J . . . That's weird. Is this a malfunction of some kind?"

When he pushed the power button on the remote, the TV would not shut down. His first thought was that the batteries needed changing. Just as he opened the device, an emergency news bulletin came on the screen. One of the twin towers in New York had been struck by an airliner.

Michael forgot all about breakfast and was glued to the set. He felt unsettled. Eventually, he made his way to the kitchen and took his morning meal to the living room. Just as he finished breaking his longer-than-normal fast, the other skyscraper was hit.

The troubled man sat by as both towers fell. While the world was watching, his inner workings needed a break. He turned off the television, grabbed his hiking stick, and went out the door. Deep into the forest and into himself, something hit him like a ton of bricks. The remote was working fine.

After the events of that one lone morning, the world would never be the same. No one knew what might happen next. During his outing, Michael's contemplations were interrupted. Birds greeted him all along the trail as reminders that all was well in their worlds.

The budding naturalist habitually talked to his fine feathered friends. Perhaps it was his imagination, but it seemed as though they were more responsive than ever.

Before he got back to the house, Michael decided to make a concentrated effort to learn more about the fowls of the air. He retrieved the bird field guide from the bookshelf beside the clock and spent several minutes familiarizing himself with the layout.

When he put it down, he picked up the TV remote. He hesitated before asking it to do its job. When he put a little pressure on the power button, the set booted right up.

Mother Pearl was very much aware that her son was troubled. How she wished to wrap her spectral arms around him. The rest of the day and into the next she tried to think of some way to soothe his spirits, but this was beyond her reach.

Mountain haunts

Fall arrived early. After days of being a news junkie, Michael needed a diversion, and the mountains were calling him. He had the luxury of venturing early in the week when there was less traffic. A day trip was a possibility, but the man with time on his hands did not wish to be rushed.

The computer novice was finding the internet a useful tool. He discovered ways to check for lodging online. Rooms were available in towns, but he was looking for something remote and rustic. Most such facilities only listed phone numbers.

Michael spent almost an hour placing calls only to learn that the cabins were booked for months. Near the bottom of the list, a proprietor told him it was his lucky day. Minutes earlier, there was a cancelation. The cottage was available for two nights during the upcoming week. And it had a hot tub.

Michael pulled a book from the shelf that he had never used. It described various mountain waterfalls and how to find them. He turned the pages, took a map, and charted a route that would take in several.

Pearly Ghost was not about to be left behind. She watched as Michael gathered both clothes and food to take along. The cabin had a kitchen and a grill. Her packing was a breeze.

Up bright and early, they were on their way. The first stop was for a breakfast prepared by someone else, a treat for Michael in itself. The next was still two hours away.

As Michael stood bundled up at the foot of a thundering waterfall, he began releasing the tension that had built up during the time of national tragedy. Thirty minutes later, the unburdening continued before another torrential cascade.

After three more waterfalls, the trusty SUV pulled into its reserved spot deep in the Smokey Mountains. The relaxation revved up when he stepped into the tub with swirling hot water.

"Michael Jonas . . . I could get used to this."

After the best night's sleep in days, he set out again. The leaves were near peak, and nature's beauty was all around him. He had already discovered that his digital camera struggled with landscapes so he focused on closeups.

Michael read again the information about an upcoming waterfall. Legend had it that three teenagers drowned there decades earlier. The locals swore the place was haunted.

The camera did a better job capturing the surging water, and the man behind the lens took several shots. The computer was left behind, so the photos would be uploaded when he returned to the cabin.

Michael routinely locked his vehicle. When he opened the door and took a seat, his eyes went immediately to the review mirror. It was pointing straight down. Had the set screw worked loose? He reached to reposition it, and the connection was very tight.

Michael felt a chill. That experience was repeated when he looked at the waterfall photos on his computer. In one, he could see the faint form of an apparition. The ghost wore green.

Part V: Heartstrings

The handyman

Michael had always been good with his hands. As a young adult, he continuously added to his collection of mechanical tools. Back when vehicles were simpler, he serviced his.

A chainsaw was an essential piece of equipment for someone living in the woods. Michael had also amassed several other handy tools.

The middle-aged man was reaching the point where he needed reading glasses. After he brought home his first pair, he was prone to put the spectacles down where he finished using them. This generated a search when he needed them again.

Walking through the woods, an idea took shape. A young cedar tree was used as a buck rub, and the scarred area had not healed over. The budding woodworker imagined taking a section, whittling out the decayed portion, and fashioning it into an eyeglass holder. It was not a difficult project, and after the finish dried, his drugstore glasses had a stylish new home.

Pearly Ghost was looking on. Before making her move, she waited until her son was in the habit of putting the reading glasses in the neat little tray. He reached for them one morning, and they were missing.

Mother Pearl watched with amusement as her son retraced his steps to see if he had resorted to his old ways. The glasses were nowhere to be found. After two days unable to locate them, he went and bought another pair.

Preparing supper late that afternoon, Michael opened the silverware drawer. His first pair was looking back at him.

"M J . . . There is no way I absentmindedly put those glasses in that drawer. Besides, I unloaded the dishwasher yesterday and they were not there then."

47

Now with two pairs, Michael had another project. Why not make a holder for each station where he most often used glasses? After some quality shop time and another drugstore run, reading glasses were within reach of the chair where he read, in the kitchen, beside his bed, and on his desk.

Mother Pearl was disappointed that Michael did not think of her. The ghost's dissatisfaction was short-lived when he took a seat, reached for a book, smiled, looked up, and said, "Thank you."

Pearly Ghost was now pleased. When Michael used his eyeglasses, would he think of her.

Ultimate Being had not paid Pearly Ghost a visit in some time. Accustomed to her suspended state of animation, it was easy to forget that it was transitory. The Divine intervened once more to set her straight.

After talking things through, the spirit was granted a continuance. She had not overstepped her bounds, and Michael was unperturbed by her presence.

Hearts rock

As a lad, some of Michael's peers collected arrowheads. He found only a couple that might have been broken ones. Rather, his eyes were drawn to heart-shaped rocks. Through the decades, his compilation had grown substantially. When he built his house, these anomalies also found a new home. The resident exhibited them atop the guard rails around his deck. Larger ones were displayed in the yard.

The collection included stones of various colors and sizes. Some were so small that Michael marveled that his eyes had spied them. He found these oddities not only on his property but in many other places where he had journeyed.

While the timing of many finds was insignificant, Michael picked up on a pattern. If he was deliberating about something, a heart rock was often in his path as a confirmation that *his heart* was in the right place.

While sipping wine one evening, Michael walked slowly around the deck revisiting when he found some of the more memorable heart rocks. He picked some up marveling at how nature formed them so nearly perfect.

Mother Pearl was attuned. She had just discovered a way to get her Angel Michael's attention.

When he was drifting off to sleep that night, a thud made him sit up in bed. It sounded like a rock fell from its perch. Had he left one in a precarious position? A floodlight with a motion sensor would have come on if a critter stumbled on it. His bed was beside the window, and the deck was dark.

The obtrusive noise gave Michael a rush, but he was too groggy to pursue it until morning. It was well up in the day before he recalled the incident. Sure enough, one of the larger stones was on the deck floor.

Pearly Ghost waited a couple of nights before duplicating her ploy. Michael shined a flashlight all around the deck area and could see no intruder. As he put his head back on the pillow, he spoke.

"Okay, you got me. I love you, too."

This heart rock mischief had far exceeded anything Mother Pearl could have foreseen. Her son just told her that he loved her.

A brush with an angel

No longer required to make himself presentable, Michael let his hair grow. It seemed like it would never get beyond the scraggly stage, but eventually, he was finally able to put it in a ponytail.

Something new was added to his daily rituals. Mornings began and days ended running a brush through his hair to get the tangles out.

About to retire for the night, Michael reached for the hairbrush, and it was missing in action. He could not remember when the brush and comb set came to live with him. Through several moves, they had always been on his bathroom counter.

The brush did not just grow legs and walk off. Neither did he walk around while stroking his silver locks. The man always stood in the same place. Nevertheless, he did a thorough search of the bathroom. It was not in any drawer or the linen closet.

Michael retrieved a smaller travel-size brush from his toiletry bag. This would make do until he could do better.

Sometimes weeks passed between Pearly Ghost's exploits, and Michael did not immediately think of her when something was amiss. This time was no different. After several days of struggling with the provisional brush, wondering if he needed to go ahead and purchase a new one, it finally hit him. He repeated words similar to what he uttered before.

"If you are through playing with my brush, I would like to have it back. But please put it in a place where I will know for certain that I had nothing to do with its disappearance."

Two weeks went by, and the brush had not reappeared. Michael came home from the grocery store with a passel of sweet potatoes. He remembered reading that they baked well in a slow cooker. He brought his crockpot from the pantry and removed the lid. The hairbrush was inside just waiting to be found.

Mother Pearl was especially proud of herself. When Michael stroked his hair, perhaps, he would be reminded of her.

A hearty maneuver

Fashioning the eyeglass holders nudged Michael into a new hobby. Wood had always fascinated him, and he was ready to take his efforts to another level.

A large burl on a maple tree kept turning his head. He imagined transforming it into an interesting bowl. After putting fresh gas in his saw and sharpening the chain, he set out to begin the project. Slicing it from the trunk of the storied old tree proved quite a challenge, but eventually, the cancerous growth was ready to take to the shop.

The greenhorn figured out quickly that he did not have the right tools for this job. When he came back from the hardware store, he addressed his partner.

"Michael Jonas . . . This will be an expensive bowl. But then again, we'll have these tools around for future jobs."

Mother Pearl was intrigued by what Michael was doing. Chips flew as the innards were churned out. Having gone about as deep into the gnarly wood piece as he dared, the neophyte stepped back.

"Just look at that."

The way the burl wrapped around the tree had shaped it like a heart. Michael meticulously trimmed the insides getting the irregular growth patterns as smooth as possible. This was not a one-day job, and darkness was prevailing. After several more work sessions, the artisan decided it was time for the proverbial artist to put down the big paintbrush and work on the trim.

When the polyurethane touched the surface, the asymmetrical woodgrain sprang to life. Michael was in awe.

"Wow!"

After two more coats were applied and they dried, the bowl was ready to take inside.

"M J . . . That is one magnificent piece of wood. I am so honored that my hands touched it."

Michael placed it on the dining table, but he was not satisfied with it there. Neither did he like it on the coffee table. Still deciding where to put it, the budding craftsman looked around. He decided that it would show off its shape and splendor much better hanging on a wall.

The woodworker attached a hanger and decided to put it behind his favorite chair. Using the stud finder, reminded him of the experience that confirmed the presence of a spirit. Pearly Ghost had not forgotten, either.

The one-of-a-kind conversation piece found its home. When Michael came from the dining room into the lounge area, it was eye-catching.

Michael strolled into the den a few days later, and it did not feel right. He panned the area but could not figure out what was niggling at him. Something was missing, but since it had not been there for very long, he did not notice it at first. Then, it hit him. The decorative heart bowl behind his chair was missing.

It did not take long to locate it. The wood piece was on the floor behind his chair. A quick check revealed that the catch on the back and the hanger on the wall were steadfastly in place. Gravity had nothing to do with its fall.

For once, there was no second-guessing himself. Michael's mind went straight to the resident poltergeist. Even so, he did not immediately make the heart connection. When he did, his face had trouble containing a big smile.

Mother Pearl could only ponder. When Michael looked up at the heart-shaped burl bowl, might he feel her love?

Heartaches

Michael made monthly calls to check on his parents. His dad seemed to be holding up well. The man had hired outside help with the housework.

It was hard to get a reading on his mother. Michael feared that his father might be in denial regarding the seriousness of her condition. Or, was the oldest son intentionally left out of the loop?

On reflective walks, he reevaluated the days of his youth. Was his mom just not cut out for affection? Michael was forced to admit that he was envious of some boyhood friends. Most mothers were actively engaged in their sons' lives and exuded pride in their growing boys' achievements.

Then, there were his siblings. Still not gushy, his mother was more involved in their activities. They had connections that eluded him. Feeling like an outsider was his normal.

Michael's heart ached, knowing that his mother was now beyond his grasp. He did not make the rules, but he must play by them. Would he ever have another chance to tell her that he loved her?

Mother Pearl kept pace with her son's yearnings as he chronicled his thoughts. She felt just as much out of his reach as his other mother was.

The contemplative man stopped before the little waterfall before moving on. His mind was seeking a way to put things in perspective.

"M J . . . It was not as though I displeased the woman. She rarely criticized me. I guess it was good that I did not need her approval."

He paused, looked up, and smiled.

"At least, no one ever called me a mama's boy."

Mother Pearly Ghost begged to differ. Her heart was now the one breaking. Would she ever find a way to show her son how much she loved him?

Part VI: Power points

The tool man

Michael looked down at his hiking stick and addressed his sidekick.

"Michael Jonas . . . You can do better than that."

Soon after declaring that he was self-unemployed, he picked up a fallen limb and trimmed it a bit. The crude staff served him well, but it was high time to deem it retired.

The amateur woodworker had been admiring a dogwood with a vine growing around it. The honeysuckle had forged groves into the trunk as it circled while climbing. Michael cut the sapling and took it to the shop.

The first step was removing the bark. Pearly Ghost looked on. The vine had just about choked the life out of the young tree. As a result, the wood contained interesting coloration patterns.

Sections of the climbing plant came right out, but other segments were tight. Michael reached for a rotary tool with a small grinding bit. When he plugged it in, the device sprang to life.

Thankfully, he had a good grip. Michael chided himself for being careless. He could have easily put pressure on the simple on/off switch when unwrapping the cord.

The new stick was set aside to cure before sanding and finishing. Meanwhile, Michael had caught the woodworking bug. He went to the woods and wandered off the beaten trail. Not sure what he was looking for, his eyes eventually strayed to an unusual growth on a cherry tree. The bark was all swelled and blistered.

"M J . . . I suspect there is some interesting and colorful grain inside. This might make a cute little bowl."

Michael took it home, studied the wood oddity, and eventually decided where to begin working. He plugged in a grinder, and it almost jumped out of his hand.

"Whoa! Is the switch malfunctioning?"

He turned the electrical tool on and off several times, and it worked properly. Not wanting to rush the project, he set it aside after about an hour. Several things distracted him before returning to it a few days later.

Digging into the flaky bark to get to the gnarly wood was the next step. He selected a tool with a stiff wire brush and plugged it in. It almost jumped off the workbench.

In some things, the man was a quick study. In others, he was a slow learner. While toiling away, his brain finally found a cog and got in gear.

"So . . . It was you. Are you having fun? Has it occurred to you that I might get hurt?"

Thereafter, Michael was meticulous to check the switch before plugging in a power tool. Not once did he again find anything already in the start position.

Birthday greens

"M J . . . Where did that year go?"

Michael woke up on his birthday ready to celebrate two recent accomplishments. His new hiking stick was ready for its maiden voyage, and a neat little cherry bowl was on the sofa-side table as a present to himself.

"No birthday blues for this birthday boy."

Rain was in the forecast, so he decided to check the weather and see if there was time to get out ahead of it. As he opened the notebook computer, the screen remained blank. The electronic device had celebrated several birthdays of its own, and Michael feared that it might have crashed. When he pushed the power button, he was relieved that it started booting up.

He knew that he did not shut it down. If there was a power fluctuation, the battery would have kicked in. Perhaps, it installed updates during the night that required rebooting.

Michael waited as the computer jumped through its hoops. When it completed its tasks, a message appeared suddenly on the screen. His eyes beheld a greeting in bold green letters.

"Happy Birthday."

Memories of a year earlier surged. The gremlin had struck again.

Mother Pearl tried to come up with a way for her son to know that the greeting was from her, but everything went right over the birthday boy's head.

The Gathering

Michael was not exactly surprised when the phone call came. His dad was convening the clan to discuss the family situation going forward. Pearly Ghost hitched a ride and listened in.

The patriarch shared the plan. It had reached the point where he was no longer able to care for his wife and their mother. The couple was moving into assisted living after the first of the year. The modern facility had different residential levels ranging from a retirement village to a nursing home. When their mother must be moved to the latter, he would relocate to the retirement wing where he could visit her regularly.

The weathered man assured his children that their parents would not be a financial burden. Years earlier, he purchased insurance to cover this possibility. In addition, the house was already on the market.

The man's offspring listened intently as he explained that they could take only necessary furnishings. The children could have whatever household items they wanted before the rest was disposed of.

Michael put in a request for only one thing. His basement doubled as a storm shelter, and he had intended to put a bed down there. He wanted his old boyhood bedroom suite.

After getting the nod, Michael mentioned something else. He assured his dad that his basement was plenty large if he wanted to store some things that he did not wish to part with. The man thanked him and promised to keep that in mind.

In the meantime, visits with their mom were to be limited. He did not think the confusion was good for her. They would forego any holiday get-togethers.

Michael wondered if he might get to see the mother who raised him. As the meeting was dispersing, his father went to her room, came back, and said that she was sleeping. They all circled her bed, and no one spoke.

On the drive back home, Mother Pearl realized how distraught her son was. It worked before, so she tried it again. The spirit applied gentle pressure to his shoulders and upper back. Without warning, he spoke.

"M J . . . I'm feeling better about all of this. Both of my parents will receive the attention they need. Wish I could do more, but that door seems closed."

Michael called his parents on Christmas Day. His dad was busy sorting through stuff ahead of the big move. The man was going out of his way to avoid any mention of the red-letter day.

Feeling like he was a nuisance, Michael was wrapping up the conversation when his father intervened. He asked his son if he was serious when offering his basement for storage. Of course, he was.

"Since a truck must come your way to bring the bedroom suite, I'll also send some furniture that I might need when I move to the retirement home. That way, I'll not have to put it in a storage unit. If it is okay with you, your brother will rent a small truck and bring them your way."

"Just let me know when he will be arriving."

Fireworks

On New Year's Eve, Michael was up later than usual watching a football game. He could hear sporadic fireworks and wished for those enjoying them something special to celebrate.

Although his house was very secluded, he felt no need for a security system, especially after installing the bars over the basement and garage windows. Nonetheless, he did have an early warning apparatus. Monitors beside the driveway and sidewalk signaled if something passed by. They were motion activated and set high enough that smaller critters went undetected. When a vehicle, person, or larger animal went by, the in-house receiver alerted with a two-note chime.

Before retiring for the night, the chirping began pealing continuously. Likely, deer were standing in front of a sending unit. When it did not stop, Michael went to investigate.

The outside units had a red light that blinked when something set them off. He could see from the dark guest bedroom window that the signal was coming from the one guarding the walk. That area was also protected by sensitive motion detector floodlights, and they had not come on.

The chiming went silent, and Michael went back to bed puzzled. While meditating on the significance of turning over yet another new leaf and with louder fireworks in the distance, the tone started ringing again. Michael manually turned on the floodlights, and he could see nothing in the front yard. Wondering if there was a malfunction, he went back to bed when the warning device eventually stopped.

Just before midnight, the grand finale fireworks of the closest neighbors woke Michael up. Meanwhile, the monitor began chirping nonstop. He shined a high-powered flashlight all around the front yard area. Nothing was moving that he could see. Convinced of an equipment failure, he turned the system off so that he could get some rest.

Relaxing to go back to sleep, it occurred to him that there might be another explanation. At that moment, he heard a confirming noise in the house and felt goosebumps. He reactivated the system the following morning, and it had no glitches. No longer feeling foolish when he addressed his poltergeist, Michael spoke aloud.

"Thank you, for helping me ring out the old and ring in a new year full of hope and promise by providing the fireworks. How very clever of you."

Just as he finished the last sentence, the monitor registered a single chime. In broad daylight, nothing was apparent that might have triggered it.

Pearly Ghost had a new toy, and she was enjoying playing with it. The next day, Michael compiled a very thoughtful and somewhat emotional email to send to a special friend navigating through some rough spots. He walked away mulling it over to make sure that he was doing the right thing. Just as he sat down at the computer, the alarm device registered a single note. Someone had sent him a ringing endorsement.

Candle power

Michael came home from the library with a handful of books. He was averse to bright lights on winter nights, preferring the lamp beside his chair. He was also prone to have a candle burning while he was reading.

One night when he got up to stretch his legs and take a bathroom break, he came back into the lounge area, and the candle had gone out.

"Michael Jonas . . . That's odd. It did not drown in a buildup of liquid wax, and the circulating air from the heat coming on has never blown it out."

He relit the candle and returned to the mystery. Without realizing it, he soon read himself to sleep. On the way to bed without wanting to become fully awake, he snuffed out the candle. When he turned off the bedroom lamp, he could see a faint glow coming from the other part of the house.

Knowing that he would never get to sleep without investigating the light, he tiptoed back through the house. Just as he came into the living room, a candle was extinguished.

"I'm not that comfortable with you playing with fire. I'm afraid you might set something ablaze."

Pearly Ghost took the rebuke in the spirit that it was intended. The last thing she wanted was to burn the house down. To let Michael know that she understood, she relit the candle and quickly extinguished it.

Her effort was not very convincing. Michael did not sleep soundly that night while Mother Pearl looked around for other ways to play with her son.

On the first Saturday of the new year, Michael helped his brother unload the truck. After his bed was set up and the other items were inside the basement, his younger sibling brought in a couple of cardboard boxes.

"These are old tax records and such that Dad did not have time to go through. He said it was doubtful that he would ever need anything, but he did not want to throw this stuff away just in case."

As the truck went up the drive, the monitoring device was on the job. After the vehicle had time to turn onto the road, Michael did a double take. It registered another single chime.

"M J . . . What was that all about?"

Power nap

Michael once laughed at those who took siestas, but that all changed when he became self-unemployed. He routinely nodded off for ten minutes or so and woke up refreshed.

This was one of Pearly Ghost's favorite times. Her apparition danced for him, and she loved hovering and looking right into his face. Mother Pearl made a game of anticipating when her son would arouse, and vanish just as he opened his eyes.

One cold winter day, Michael's power nap was more than just a catnap. He went into a deep sleep that lasted almost half an hour. Mother Pearl finished her antics and savored moments just watching him.

As Michael was coming back around, he had an eerie feeling that somebody was in the house. His sensations were on edge when he opened his eyes abruptly. Mother Pearl was careless. Her apparition was standing before him.

"Please don't go."

Michael watched as the figure faded. The female ghost was adorned in a green cloak.

After the chills subsided, Michael was thrilled. He always believed that his poltergeist was the spirit of a woman. Now, it was confirmed. Her image was indelibly imprinted into the recesses of his memory bank.

But who was she? Did she have some kind of connection with him? Michael was as mystified as ever.

Pearly Ghost was conflicted. Might this misstep bring about the demise of her visitation? She did not have to wait long to find out. Ultimate Truth soon made an appearance.

"What do you have to say for yourself?"

"I was careless. Please forgive me."

"My mercy is inexhaustible. That is not the issue here."

The humbled spirit tried again.

"The only thing different is that Michael now knows my gender, which he already suspected. He still has no inkling regarding the circumstances of his birth."

Even in a state where time was no more, the pause seemed everlasting. After thoroughly assessing the situation, Pearly Ghost received still another reprieve with the admonition to be more careful. That was an ongoing trial.

Part VII: Mothers

The Gulf

Pearly Ghost was torn. More than anything, she wanted Michael to know who she was and that she loved him. Nevertheless, if he found out, her time with him would likely be up. He was right there within her grasp, and yet, he was so unreachable. For the time being, she decided to hold herself in reserve.

Michael was at a loss about what to do for his mother. He wished so much to visit her during a period of lucidity. It seemed like some invisible gulf was keeping them apart. For now, he must bide his time.

Walking through the woods, Michael reached down and retrieved a lighter knot.

"M J . . . Your grandpa used these to get a fire going."

Not knowing exactly why, he took the piece of fatwood home with him. He picked it up later, and an idea was born. If he squared one end and drilled out the other, it would make an interesting pencil/pen holder.

Before putting tools to work, Michael checked carefully to see if the switches were in the off position. Each was. Mother Pearl watched curiously. The resin-rich piece of wood gummed up the bits, but slowly and surely, the insides came out. Long cured, it was soon ready for a finishing coat.

The practical piece dried slowly, but eventually, the woodworker took the holder inside. It replaced a nondescript one that he had used for years.

The first time Michael reached for a pen, it was missing. A couple of pencils and a highlighter were right where he placed them.

Pearly Ghost had behaved long enough. He did the usual mental exercises to see if he could remember using the writing instrument and perhaps putting it down somewhere.

"Michael Jonas . . . You have scribbled nothing since you put that pen in its new home."

He looked in the desk drawers to no avail. Needing to sign a document and get it in the mail, he found another ballpoint pen.

When Michael went to his desk to boot up the computer the next morning, two pens were among the other items in the holder.

"I love you, too."

Mother Pearl swooned. This was the second time her son told her that he loved her. At least for a brief slice of eternity, that boundless divide did not seem so unfathomable.

Too

Pearly Ghost was running low on whims. Then, she came up with a new game. The spirit watched when Michael was finishing up in the kitchen. After he walked away, she opened just a bit the last drawer that he was in.

The poltergeist remained on guard for when he might return to the kitchen. The phantom was gleeful when he nonchalantly pushed it shut. A day or so later, she pulled the same stunt with a cabinet door, and she got the same result.

Over the next couple of weeks, Pearly Ghost alternated between drawers and cabinets, pausing for a day or so now and then. She could not always read his mind, but she understood his words.

"M J . . . Are you getting senile? Why can't you remember to close things?"

It took a while, but Michael eventually put two and two together.

"I don't suppose you have anything to do with this, do you?"

Mother Pearl was ecstatic. When Michael rolled out of bed the next morning and headed to the kitchen to kickstart the coffee pot, every cabinet door was slightly ajar and each drawer was open a tad. Thinking of his mother's condition, he was relieved to know that he was not losing his mind.

The ghoul was once again fresh out of ideas. As Michael was unloading groceries, a juicy one popped into her ethereal head. He had brought home a frozen pizza. Two days later, she heard her son addressing his inner child.

"M J . . . That pizza is like money burning a hole in my pocket."

Mother Pearl made her first move. She looked on as Michael read the directions. They indicated the unlikelihood that the pizza would drip, but putting a cookie sheet under it as a precaution, was a good idea.

Before turning on the oven to preheat, the cook reached for the large flat pan. It was not in the cabinet where he kept it. Michael began a thorough search of the kitchen and could not locate it.

"I used the baking sheet last week when I made oatmeal cookies. I remember distinctly putting it up after washing it. Oh, well. It's doubtful that it will drip anyway."

When the stove indicated that the oven was preheated, Michael opened the door. The baking pan was on the lower shelf.

"Did I put it back in the oven after I washed it?"

Pearly Ghost was not through. The next time Michael put his keys, change, and knife in his pocket, they went down his leg and fell on the floor.

"Michael Jonas . . . How did that pocket come to have such a big hole in it?"

In a hurry, he selected another pair. That night, he took his sewing kit and clumsily did a patch job. Then, it hit him. He had compared the pizza to burning a hole in his pocket.

He looked up as though his friendly ghost was watching. She was.

"I love you, too."

There . . . He said it again.

"He said, 'I love you, too.' *Too*? Was my son acknowledging that he knows I love him?"

Mother's Day

Michael dreaded making calls to check on his parents. It was never a convenient time. His dad was always right in the middle of something, or he said he could hear his wife calling from the other room.

Mother's Day was approaching, and Michael was fettered. His first thought was to send flowers, but that was such a feeble token. As the day got closer, he made a decision.

"M J . . . You must do your part whether anyone else does or not. Back your ears and go see your mother."

Michael picked up a floral arrangement to hand deliver. Cut flowers would not last very long so he decided on a greenery pot. Mother Pearl was pleased with his choice. Not sure if his parents might attend a religious service, he waited until after lunch. Pearly Ghost equivocated but decided to go along.

The oldest son was on unfamiliar turf when the SUV found a parking place near the assisted living wing. Michael did not know the number of the residence, so he went straight to the desk.

The attendee asked who had come to visit, and what his relationship was. Michael answered, and the woman looked in her files.

"I'm sorry, but you are not on the pre-approved list."

Michael stepped back. What? Was he being denied access to his parents?

Realizing the consternation, the assistant glanced up at what he was carrying and volunteered to call the apartment.

"Maybe it was just an oversight on somebody's part."

Michael and Pearly Ghost could only hear one side of the conservation.

"Yes."

"Michael."

"He says he's your son."

Pause

"And he has brought something for his mom on Mother's Day."

She turned to Michael.

"Please have a seat. He's on his way."

Michael's mind was all over the place, but he would not let it find mooring until he heard what his father had to say.

"Why did you come without calling first?"

"I wanted to surprise Mother with this arrangement."

"She does not handle surprises very well."

Michael's dad was between the old proverbial rock and a hard spot. He did not wish to hurt his adopted son's feelings, but there was a great risk that his wife might lose her discretion. Backed into a corner, he hoped for the best.

Neither man spoke as they walked through the winding hallways. That no words were uttered was no indication of idle thoughts.

Michael's dad was once more second-guessing the long-ago decision not to tell their son that he was adopted. He always yielded to his wife. She feared if Michael knew the truth that he might daydream about living with an idealized image of his birth mother and reject her.

Michael's head was spinning. Must he have special permission just to visit his parents? Were there missing pieces to this puzzle?

The son stood by as his dad took the key that he must wear on a chain around his neck and unlocked the door. Once inside, he turned to Michael.

"Here, I'll take that."

Michael meekly handed over the pot and watched as it was placed on the kitchen counter.

"Let me check on your mother. She might be asleep."

Michael watched as his father closed the door behind him. He was gone for several minutes before coming back out.

"She wanted to make herself presentable."

Michael followed his father. The person sitting in the chair hardly resembled the woman who raised him. The progressive brain disease was taking its toll on other bodily functions as well.

His dad yielded. Michael was not sure what his mother was told about his visit. He went over and leaned in.

"Happy Mother's Day."

"Is that you, David? You look nothing like your brother."

"No, Mother, it's me . . . Michael."

"David . . . You were such a good boy. I have always been so proud of you. Do you know how much I love you?"

"I love you, too, Mother."

Mother Pearl shed ghostly tears. No mention was made of the greenery he brought.

Michael's mind went into overdrive on the way back home.

"Michael Jonas . . . Have you been edited out of your family's manuscript?"

Mother Superior

Michael felt a wave of melancholy wash over him. Without conscious thought, he went to the bookcase and pulled out his old high school senior yearbook. Memories jumped about like jackrabbits. Without saying it aloud, he was looking for reasons why he was not the kind of son that his parents would be proud of.

The shroud of gloom had a hard time lifting. It began slowly relenting when he was looking at the photos of his schoolmates. He had kept up with very few of his old friends, but that did not stop the former student from pausing for choice recollections from back in the day. He dated three of the girls but was not in love with any of them.

Faculty shots sent his mind spinning. He had no way of knowing which side of the green pastures they were on now. Michael also conjectured about how many of his classmates had gone on to glory. He had attended no class reunions.

While working his way through the clubs and activities sections with Mother Pearl looking on, he came to the two pages that covered the senior play. It was hard to imagine ever being in that role. As he recalled, his parents did not attend either performance.

About to let that thought derail him, he closed the yearbook and went looking for his hiking stick. It was not in its standard place. Michael remembered parking it out on the trail while using both hands to photograph a hawk perched in a tall oak watching him. Perhaps, he walked away and left it.

That thought prompted him to go back inside and get his pocket camera. When he got to the place where he thought he might have left the stick, it was not there. A wren lit on a limb just ahead.

"Sing me a song."

Michael turned on the video and recorded Jenny Wren singing her little heart out. That device was unable to detect that it was a duet.

Pearly Ghost further perused the annual during the night. She was delighted that her offspring was an officer in several clubs. He played both baseball and basketball. Mother Pearl was especially amused to find out that her son was voted most likely to be an astronaut.

After turning another page, the proud mother let out a ghoulish glee.

"My boy was a leading man."

After breakfast, Michael continued the stroll down memory lane. His mother's spirit was a silent observer as he thoughtfully translated his feelings into words.

Pearly Ghost stumbled with her recollections. She could not recall her schooling, or even what it was like to give birth. At that moment in time, she did not have the foggiest notion about the boy's father.

Equally vague was why she was unable to raise her son. Important was that she was enjoying him now. Somewhere in the corner of a recess, the ghost got a glimpse of once being a nun.

"For some reason, I was not the one Michael called mom, but I will always be his Mother Superior."

That was settled once and for all for her, but Michael was still disquieted. Out the door, he went. When he returned to the house, his hiking stick was back by the basement door.

Moving day

Michael was not surprised when his brother called and said that he was on his way to pick up the things stored in the basement. The family had known for some time that their mother was soon ready to go into the nursing home.

"M J . . . Except for the stored furnishings, I don't suppose that I would have known anything about the move."

The brothers talked some while loading the truck. David said that their dad was looking forward to moving into the retirement village.

"He has been so confined that he had little in the way of a social life."

"That man will make friends. There is no doubt about that."

"Yes. And I do hope he finds enjoyment as he begins this new chapter in his life."

As the truck left the yard, Michael was in no hurry to do anything. He stood for a few moments soaking up the summer sun and basking in the gentle breezes. All of a sudden, he thought of something. Nothing was said about the two cardboard boxes over in the corner. They were not in his way and could just stay put.

As Michael took a step to move on, his eyes were drawn to his feet. In plain sight was a beautiful heart-shaped stone.

"Wow! I have walked right along here hundreds of times and never noticed that rock."

Michael put it in his pocket to add to his collection, making sure that it did not slide down his leg. Reentering the lower part of his house, he felt a loss when he looked at the empty spaces.

"Michael Jonas . . . Your old bed might well be the only link still connecting you to your family roots."

No storm clouds were on the horizon, but Michael spent his first night in the basement. He was not alone. As he approached his boyhood bed to retire, the covers were already turned down.

Mother Earth

Michael knew "chef" would never be a part of his legacy. Nonetheless, he got by fairly well cooking for himself. He had expanded the little herb garden to include more varieties and added tomatoes and peppers. The deer prevented growing anything else.

Past the risk of a late freeze, it was time to set out some plants. Playing in the dirt was just the therapy that Michael needed. He took material from his compost heap and began working it into the soil. Spading up earthworms was a good sign.

"M J . . . Mother Earth is moaning and groaning. Her over-populous offspring are putting just about more on the old gal than she can bare."

Michael's thoughts went to his mother. Soon, the body housing her spirit would be recycled back into the dirt from which it was composed. He presumed that his parents would be buried in the same cemetery as his grandparents. The oldest son wondered if anyone would even let him know when the time came.

Living alone, well almost alone, Michael was prone to talk to himself. The upcoming discourse went well beyond how he typically addressed his M J cohort.

Troubling thoughts finally made their way to the surface. Mother Pearl was listening in. She could not remember what became of her earthly remains.

"Why did I become such a bother to my mother? What was the tipping point?"

After waiting for an answer that never came, Michael dug deeper.

"Did I have anything to do with the onset and progression of her Alzheimer's?"

A drop of rain invaded his thoughts.

"Oh, good. Mother Nature will water these plants for me."

Mother Pearl had thoughts of her own.

"My precious son . . . I hope and pray that I never become a burden for you."

Part VIII: Suzy Q

A Green Christmas

Mother Pearl became somewhat detached from Michael's daily routines. On warm days, he loved to be outside. Her son went places that she had no interest in. The ghost's biggest concern was doing something that might cause him to question his intellectual abilities. She knew that he had not inherited anything from the mother he knew, but he didn't.

Michael went about with little thought of his poltergeist. He did smile occasionally when he put his knife in his pocket. Pearly Ghost's antics were spaced out far enough that he did not automatically think of her.

One thing continued to puzzle him. Who was she? Was the specter somebody who once lived on his property? If so, why was he getting all of this attention?

There was one other possibility. Was the ghost someone from his past? Might this be the spirit of a girl that he was once in love with? So far as he knew, the ones on that shortlist were all still alive.

Could she be family? Other than his grandmothers, he had lost no immediate female kin. He was not close to either, and both were deceased several years before the visitations began.

Michael wondered if he would ever know. It was consoling that he had a friendly ghost. She still made the hairs stand up on his arms and back, but he had no generalized fear of her.

This was not something that he could share in casual conversation. He might as well say that he was abducted by a space alien. If this was not happening to him, he would be a skeptic, too. Were his schoolmates prophetic when they voted him the most likely to be an astronaut? Was this other resident an alien from outer space?

Pearly Ghost read all about it. She especially liked the space alien part.

Michael's thoughts turned to the holidays. He heard nothing from anybody back home during Thanksgiving Week. Not in a cooking mood, he could just make do.

"Michael Jonas . . . One thing I'm most thankful for is that I don't get caught up in other folks' messy stuff."

As Christmas approached, he so much wished for an overture. The jilted son knew better than to just show up again unannounced.

He and his brother were on civil terms. Michael called but had to leave a message on voice mail and heard nothing back until the next day. David told him that no holiday plans had been made. Their mother was steadily losing ground, and their father did not think visits were helpful. Michael wondered if he was the only one being blocked.

"My old pal, M J . . . We will have ourselves a merry little Christmas."

Christmas dinner revolved around a butt section of ham that Michael smoked. He sampled it ahead of time and was very pleased. Cranberry and potato salads were waiting in the fridge as side dishes. The chief cook and bottle washer also wanted something green to round out the simple meal.

Certain that a can of green beans was in the pantry, he went to retrieve it on Christmas Eve. Michael had saved the ham juices from the smoker's water pan and was looking forward to drizzling some on the beans.

To his disappointment, he could not find what he was looking for. He moved everything around to make sure his eyes were not overlooking the can.

Michael searched again the next morning with the same results. Two other greens were in the pantry, and he chose spinach over collards. He was saving the latter for New Year's Day. As the recluse savored the modest Christmas dinner, the drippings on the spinach gave it a gentle boost.

"M J . . . Sometimes simple is just awesome."

Three days after Christmas, the culinary improviser carved enough pieces of ham for another meal, a ham and cheese sandwich, two ham biscuits, and ham and eggs. The time had come to slice the remainder, vacuum seal it, and freeze it for future meals.

The hambone was not tossed. Michael plugged in the crockpot. Over the bone not trimmed too closely, he added more of the flavor-rich stock. After chopping celery, carrots, and onion, he went to the pantry to bring out a variety of canned tomatoes and vegetables for the promise of some exceptional soup. Sitting right there in plain sight was a can of Jolly Green Giant green beans.

Pearly Ghost had celebrated yet another green Christmas.

A hot date

Michael was surprised when he received a call from an old high school chum. The students called her Suzy Q. The woman said she was looking through yearbooks and wondered what he was up to.

"How did you find me?"

"Michael . . . You'd be surprised by how much the internet knows about all of us. It didn't take long for me to track you down."

"Where are you calling from?"

"As it turns out, I live only about a half hour from you."

"Want to come over sometime and continue this conversation?"

"Just say when. I already know your address, and my GPS can find you."

Michael had been contemplating building a campfire for some time, and Suzy's upcoming visit was just the spark he needed. It was Good Friday, and that made it more special. She arrived in time to help get wieners ready for roasting and marshmallows set aside for toasting. Mother Pearl watched as Michael took his pocketknife and cut forked sticks.

There was a chill in the early spring air. The roaring fire provided good warmth just so long as the backyard picnickers kept doing their best imitation of a rotisserie. Making conversation, Michael spoke.

"You were in the class behind me."

"That's right. I probably shouldn't tell you this, but I had a crush on you."

"Really? Is that why you looked me up?"

"Maybe."

It was now his turn. Dare he?

"I was once a little sweet on you, too."

"Too bad, you never let me know."

Pearly Ghost was taking notes.

Playing with fire

Waiting for the fire to burn down, Michael and Suzy were mesmerized by the flames. Each kept poking it. She spoke first.

"It's not hard to understand why primitive people associated fire and smoke with spirits. As the plumes rise, you don't have to stretch your imagination much to see ghostly figures."

"Holy Smoke. There is so much more to the spirit world than what we know."

"Michael . . . Do you believe in ghosts?"

"Why do you ask?"

"Just curious. Something tells me you do."

"Do you?"

"Certainly not the Hollywood version."

"What then?"

"I don't know. The subject fascinates me, but I've never had any personal experience."

"The coals are just right. Let's get on with the program before we get cold."

Michael left the door open for a quip about him keeping Suzy warm, but she did not take the bait. After an enchanting meal with some enthralling conversation, the two repacked the picnic basket and returned to the house.

Suzy went to the guest bathroom but soon came back out.

"Have you seen my comb?"

"What does it look like? But no, I haven't."

"It's larger than your run-of-the-mill comb. I used it before I left my condo, and I know I put it back in my purse. You didn't seem to mind what I looked like in the dim glow. You'll just have to get used to my Gipsy look."

"I'll just turn on some dim lamplight. Anyway . . . Windblown is earthy and unpretentious."

"Michael . . . You always were so polite."

The host walked his guest to the car, but without his coat, he did not tarry. His ears were perked to hear the driveway monitor, but it did not register in. He went to the window to watch for taillights just as there was a knock at the door. Suzy was on the other side holding up a large comb.

"Come back inside and tell me about it."

"Michael . . . I did not use that comb on the way here, and there is no way it fell out of my purse. It was zipped. Were you messing with me? I've never known you to be a practical joker."

"Let me assure you that I had nothing to do with it. For one thing, I've never gone into any woman's purse, and I'm not about to start now."

"Well, it's a mystery. I'm just glad to have it back. I've had it for years, and it's like a security blanket. Goodnight, again."

As the monitor chimed this time, Michael smiled.

"So . . . You like Suzy Q."

Moments

On Easter Sunday, Michael called his dad. The man said that he was doing fine and making new friends. Two meals a day were provided, so he had to only manage breakfast. When asked, he said that hospice would be called in soon to help care for his wife. Pearly Ghost was suspended right over the phone trying to hear both sides of the conversation.

Michael walked away wishing for a contact that he could count on. Not much was left of his mother's mind. For the first time, he realized that he had seen her for the last time.

Mother Pearl wished to comfort her son. She accompanied him on a long walk into the woods. Michael paused at the little cascading waterfall. His birth mother added to the soothing.

He remembered the last picture taken of him and his mother. How it got in his camera remained a mystery.

As the worshipful man turned to leave, his head reversed course. His eyes had spotted a white heart-shaped rock in the creek. He retrieved it, held it high, and looked up.

"Thank you, Lord."

Michael decided to build another fire and roast fish over the coals. That seemed like an Easter kind of thing to do. His thoughts inevitably returned to the last fire in the pit. He wondered if Suzy Q's curiosity was filled.

"Michael Jonas . . . What are the odds that you will ever hear from her again?"

After they discussed ghosts around the campfire and then the comb incident, he suspected that he would. He was pleased that they exchanged email addresses.

Michael routinely checked his computer for late-breaking news and possible messages before bedtime. One popped up from Suzy. He was not the only one reading it.

His recent guest again thanked her host for a lovely evening. She went on to say that the most surprising part of the visit was how Michael did not quiz her about her past. Neither did he go into details regarding his. Suzy closed with a comment suggesting how nice it was just to live in those moments.

"M J . . . About the only thing you learned about her is that she works at the library. But she sure does seem to be a nice person."

Kitchen capers

With full access to the whole house, Mother Pearl preferred hanging out in the kitchen. The nun never had a kitchen of her own.

Like everyone else, her son had his routines. One was to sprinkle cinnamon and ginger on toast and oatmeal. The tins were twins and had side-by-side spots in the spice cabinet.

When he reached for them one morning, the cinnamon was missing. They always went in and out as a pair, but their bond was now broken.

"M J . . . Were you distracted with it in your hand? Did the phone ring or someone come to the door? Did you unthinkingly put it down somewhere?"

Michael did a thorough search that came up empty. When he next bought groceries, ginger got a new partner. As he put the cinnamon tin in the cabinet, he mumbled to himself.

"I think the old one was about empty anyway."

Mother Pearl was disappointed that she got no credit. Her next coy ploy would certainly get Michael's attention. Needing to lightly grease a skillet, he reached for the olive oil aerosol.

Something did not feel right in his hand. Just in the nick of time, he took his finger off the nozzle before spraying green paint on the pot. For once, Michael did not go sniffing around for a rational explanation.

"Nice one. But I think I'll keep the skillet its original color."

A cool date

When Michael came in from tinkering with a piece of wood, the answering machine light was blinking. Whenever the phone rang, or there was a message, he momentarily froze. Was this *the* call?

It wasn't. Suzy Q was inviting him to visit her. She said that she could not top the campfire, but candles would be burning.

"Michael Jonas . . . Why not?"

Pearly Ghost was not about to be left behind. Suzy emailed directions, and they were surprisingly simple. The thirty-minute drive was a nice diversion from thoughts weighing heavily on the driver.

Suzy's condo was in a complex with various recreational facilities and a lake. As Michael parked in a spot reserved for visitors, he wondered if he should have brought flowers or perhaps a bottle of wine.

"M J . . . I think not. That would make this something like a date."

When Suzy met him at the door, it was obvious that she had spent a considerable amount of time working on her hair. Michael's deadpan was not about to be subdued.

"I'm sorry. I'm at the wrong door. I came to visit a Gipsy woman."

"I hope you are not too disappointed. This do will have to do."

"Who said anything about being disappointed?"

Suzy Q was fun to be with. Michael remembered what she said about being in the moment. He was not into oversharing, so that meshed well.

After showing Michael around her place, they settled in the lounge area.

"Want to take a tour of my little town?"

"That would be nice."

"You'll have to drive. I'm blocked in."

Michael saw no indication of any cooking going on in the kitchen. Perhaps, they might end up at an eating establishment. When he wheeled back into her drive, he thought maybe he should have eaten before he came. Another place they did not go by was the library.

When they went back inside, and true to Suzy's promise, she lit two candles.

"How about a glass of wine?"

"Sounds cool."

"What kind do you like? Like I can give you a big choice."

"I'll have what you're having."

Michael did not know what he might say if the ghost subject came back up. As the evening wore on, Suzy showed no inclination to go there. When the glasses were drained, she sat up straight and faced him.

"The only thing that I know you like to eat is a hotdog. So, you get to choose from my stash of frozen dinners."

After an unpretentious meal with another guest looking on, a lively discussion followed touching on topics that kept bouncing around.

As Michael was sending nonverbal signals that it was time for him to leave, his hostess put the evening in perspective.

"I'm around books all day but have so little stimulating conversation. I hope we can do this again."

"The librarian is well-read. This has been very enjoyable. Let's."

Michael leaned in and kissed Suzy's hairdo.

As he opened the door of his SUV, he did a U-turn. When the doorbell rang, Suzy wondered if Michael was returning to finish what he started. Instead, he was holding a familiar object.

"You left your comb on the front seat. It must have slipped out of your purse."

Suzy was baffled when Michael told her goodnight again and left. Once his seatbelt was on, he spoke to the other passenger.

"Still having fun?"

The call

Coming in from the garage, the blinking answering machine was at it again. Could it be Suzy wanting to talk about the comb? No. It was *the call* that Michael was dreading. Anyone else might have thought it strange that it came from the funeral home.

Michael's custodial mother died peacefully after a horrific struggle. Funeral plans were incomplete. The oldest son was advised to check the establishment's website for updates.

"Michael Jonas . . . I never had *the* talk with her that I so much wished to. I didn't get to tell my mother how much I appreciated all that she did for me when I was growing up. I do hope she died knowing that I loved her as much as she allowed me to."

Talking things out with M J promoted healing. Still, Michael wanted to share the news with someone else who might be understanding.

Suzy was surprised when she saw Michael's name on the caller ID. Did he want to talk more about the mysterious comb? When he told her the reason for reaching out, the man in mourning realized that he had made the right call. He sensed caring coming through the airwaves. Suzy asked him to keep her apprised of the plans. He gave her the funeral home webpage address.

The night of the family visitation was awkward. The rest of the clan gathered around the casket. Michael greeted a smaller host of old friends over in a corner.

Pearly Ghost was apprehensive in the mortuary. The last thing she wished was to bump into the spirit of Michael's other mother. She was relieved that the evening passed without incident.

During the memorial service on the following day, Michael had a hard time focusing. He knew his mother to be a woman of high morals and principled values. The grieving son appreciated the fine things being said about her. Still, he struggled to put aside how the woman being depicted was so detached from him.

Michael drove alone to the cemetery, or at least, he thought he was by himself. After his mother's mortal remains were committed back to the earth, he turned to leave. Somebody came up from behind and reached for his hand.

Startled, Michael found himself looking into the bleary eyes of Suzy Q. Mother Pearl was looking on, but her eyes were also scanning the skies. Before Michael had time to say a word, a sharp bolt of lightning got everyone's attention. Huge raindrops began falling.

The gathering dispersed quickly. Michael held onto Suzy and took her to his SUV.

"Well, sir . . . You now get to see my wet look."

"You know what they say. Variety is the spice of life."

Suzy's expression changed.

"That lightning was close."

Michael's demeanor also morphed.

"I can see the headline."

"Wayward son struck by lightning at his mother's funeral."

"This wayward son is not going anywhere anytime soon."

Neither seemed to know what to say next. After an awkward pause, Suzy found her voice.

"Michael . . . Do you want to go somewhere and talk?"

The oldest son had overheard some discussion about the family going to his brother's house for a meal prepared by friends and neighbors, but nobody specifically invited him.

"I would like that very much."

Pearly Ghost had a choice. Which vehicle would she ride in?

A Divine moment

With no forewarning, Ultimate Love appeared before Pearly Ghost. Using the customary ethereal telepathy, the Divine suggested again that the time had come for the spirit to resume her suspended journey.

"Michael has a load off his shoulders with his other mother's passing. He is fine now."

"But I'm still not ready. Don't you agree that I have not been reckless lately?"

"I'll grant you that, but here is something for you to consider. Sometimes your pranks make Michael question his sanity. We know that he does not carry his other mother's family genes, but he doesn't."

"I'm already aware of that. I do not want to cause him unnecessary worry."

"Just be more judicious. And one more thing. Michael has a new friend. He needs all the space in the world to figure things out as he goes along. It would not be fair to him if you did something to short-circuit it."

"But I like her, and should I ever not, I promise that I will not interfere. I am so happy for Michael that he has someone to talk to and share things with."

"You have always honored your promises, and I will take that into consideration."

After a Divine moment, Pearly Ghost was once again awarded more bonus time with an admonition.

"Maybe you should curtail your activities, or you might run her off."

"I'll try."

Breathing a sigh of relief, Mother Pearl went to check on Michael. He was sitting on the deck in the stillness. Without a single leaf stirring, the wind chimes began playing a gentle melody. Michael uttered a lone syllable.

"Wow!"

Pearly Ghost was excited. Suzy Q was on her way. Michael's mother envisioned an ally in the making. He was busy tidying things up.

"M J . . . This is the first housecleaning that I've done since she was here the last time. But don't expect that woman to turn me into a tidy fanatic."

As the man's hands were busy, his mind was also fully engaged. After the memorial service, he and Suzy talked for hours. He opened up to her and shared things regarding his family that he had always bottled up. The woman was nothing but understanding and supportive.

One subject had not yet come back up. Michael was unsure how he might handle it if and when it did. He promised Suzy a walk in the woods. On that, he could deliver. Out on the trail, she put in her order for a hiking stick, and he pledged to make that happen, too.

When back inside, it was Michael's turn to offer a glass of wine. He only had one kind on hand, and it would have to do. When Suzy finished, she put the glass on the coffee table. Facing the man sitting next to her, she went straight to the point.

"Michael . . . Now, about that comb."

He knew it was coming, just not when. What came out of his mouth was unlike anything that he had ever imagined. Rising to his feet, he blurted it out.

"I need to go see a man about a dog."

That was just about the last thing Suzy anticipated, and she broke into laughter.

"I haven't heard that expression since we were back in high school. Michael . . . I'm a big girl, now. It's okay to say that you need to go to the bathroom."

"Michael Jonas . . . At least, you made her laugh."

Behind the closed door, the man must make a big decision. He had mentioned the strange happenings to two friends right after they began, but he never followed up with them. Otherwise, he had not uttered a word to anyone else about his ghost.

There was also the matter of the poltergeist. What if she objected to anyone else knowing about her? Michael did not wish to do anything that might offend her. He had been gone too long still not sure what he was going to do. Exiting the bathroom, he reached for the light switch. Just before his hand touched it, the room went dark.

"Is that a yes or a no?"

The light came back on.

"Then, yes, it is."

Part IX: Playmates

The projects

Michael meandered through the woods looking for just the right sapling to make Suzy a hiking stick. He found no others with vine scars like his. About to give up, he stumbled over a small stump that pulled him sideways. After regaining his balance, he spotted another red cedar used as a buck rub.

The little tree tried to heal from its wound, but its needles were brown. Michael saw some possibility. He cut it, trimmed the top, and walked it home.

As the woodworker scrapped off the gummy bark, he found crimson colors mingled with the natural lightness. He decided to do very little shaving where the deer had already removed the outer layer. That aged area was a contrasting medium brown.

Since the cedar had already given up the ghost, he was able to go directly to sanding. Once the polyurethane hit the various colors, the comatose stick took on a new life.

Was it the right size? Would it make a good fit? What if she didn't like it? Michael imagined Suzy's hand around the grip and decided that it just might work. The craftsman already had one vote of confidence. He just didn't know it.

Michael was re-energized. Undergrowth was overtaking his hiking trails, and the paths needed grooming. He wanted them cleared when Suzy took her first walk with her new stick.

"M J . . . This is like outdoor housework."

With his camera in one pocket and his knife in another, he made light work of the project. Curious birds dropped in to check out what he was doing.

Mother Pearl found nothing exciting about the job and went back home. Other things were on her mind. The ghost now had two playmates, and she was making plans.

As Michael clipped the invasive plants, his thoughts circled back to the lively conversation with Suzy about his poltergeist. The woman accepted what he said without hesitation or reservation. There was no doubt in his mind that the ghost was listening in, and he wondered about her reaction. She was working on it.

Pearly Ghost was stymied. She could think of all kinds of pranks involving the house, but she was looking for one specific to Suzy.

Michael's mind went on an adventure as he worked. He collected thoughts to record when he got back to the house. Mother Pearl was nosey when he sat down at the computer.

"Is there such a thing as fate? Were the Hindus right about karma? Did some guiding force make sure Suzy's path crossed mine just as Mother was going into serious decline?"

He saved the document, but the subject was by no means closed. Mother Pearl could think of nothing she could do that might provide the enlightenment her son was searching for.

The performance

Michael must work around Suzy's library schedule to spend time with her. She worked every other weekend with compensatory days that she had some choice in arranging. The upcoming Saturday, she was off and coming over.

Michael had mentioned nothing about her hiking stick. He was proud of his handiwork and hoped she would appreciate it, too.

Pearly Ghost listened in on phone conversations and was anticipating the visitor. She wanted so much to find a way to make the woman feel accepted, but she was butting her ghoulish head against the immutable proverbial wall.

Michael had given some thought about how he would hand over the stick. Perhaps, throw in some *slapstick*. Mother Pearl had no idea what he was thinking.

Michael was like a birthday boy wanting to open a present early.

"M J . . . Why do I feel like a clumsy teenager?"

Soon after Suzy Q was inside, Michael told her that he had a surprise. She was naturally intrigued. He added that before presenting it to her, there were some things he wanted to go over with her. The woman had a quizzical look, while Pearly Ghost was spellbound.

"Remember putting in your request for a hiking stick? It was not an easy order to fill, but I have one for you to consider. If you don't like it, I'll look for something else."

"I cannot imagine not liking it. Let me see it."

"Not so fast. When a woman picks out a hiking stick, it is somewhat like picking out a man."

"How so?"

"The first thing a female needs to know when selecting a staff is that *there is no such thing as a perfect stick.*"

Michael paused and watched for a reaction. A devilish look was on Suzy's face. Pearly Ghost was also enthralled.

"Most are just average run-of-the-mill sticks, but others are exceptional. Still, there are no perfect sticks. Some are big sticks, little sticks, long sticks, short sticks, ugly sticks, and pretty sticks, but none without flaws. Other sticks are straight, and some are crooked. There are rough sticks, tough sticks, and smooth sticks, but no perfect sticks."

Michael was on a roll.

"Mother Nature did not endow all sticks equally. So, when you are picking out a hiking stick, know that yours will have some imperfections. Accept your rod for what it is, and do not try to change it."

"Okay . . . Are you going to make me beg?"

"Patience, dear girl. There's more that you need to know. *Looks are not everything*. This does not mean that appearance is unimportant. You want a stick that you will be proud to have by your side. The two of you need to look good together. Nevertheless, looks are overrated."

"How so?"

"Strength and character are far more important than curb appeal. You might be tempted to pick out a staff with a lot of pizzazz, but you could be stuck with just a pretty boy stick worth little more than a conversation piece. On a strenuous hike, an ugly stick with strength and character will take much better care of you."

"Just how ugly is my stick?"

"You will be the judge of that, but hang on. I'm still not through. The third reason picking out a stick is like picking out a man is that *size really does matter*."

Suzy erupted in laughter, Pearly Ghost blushed, and Michael prattled on.

"If you are just taking the old boy around the block a time or two, any old stick will do. But if you're taking him deep into the woods and keeping him on the job for hours at a time, you will need a longer stick. When going up and down steep hills, the extra length is very important so that you can put the rod out in front and brace yourself on it."

"Are you concerned that my stick might be too long or too short?"

"If it's too long, I can cut some off. If it's too short, you will have to look elsewhere."

Before Suzy had a chance to respond, Michael continued the presentation.

"Please also know that the right size is more than just about length. The stick needs to fit just right in your hand. If it is too thick, your fingers cannot keep a good grasp. After a while, they will ache when holding onto the oversized barrel."

Mother Pearl imagined her son on a big stage giving the performance of his life. The audience roared in appreciation. Michael was about to bring the curtain down.

"If the stick is too small, your fingers will cramp as they overlap in an unnatural grip. So, the hiking stick needs to be just the right size so that your fingers wrap around it with a good snug fit. The stick also needs to have a balance point where it feels comfortable in your hand."

"Have you thought about taking this show on the road? Now, where's my damn stick?"

Michael had hidden it in the coat closet. He brought it out and handed it over.

"Well, what do you think?"

"It's *almost* perfect . . . Just like you."

Mother Pearl smiled when Michael's face turned the same color as the crimson in the cedar wood.

The prank

Pearly Ghost just could not grasp how to put her stamp of approval on Suzy. The kitchen was still her best proving ground, but she could think of nothing that directly involved the woman.

Meanwhile, Mother Pearl was getting over a little spectral snit about sharing her kitchen with Michael's friend. What she wanted most was for her son to be happy.

Michael was getting worried. It was unlike his friendly ghost to go silent for very long with so much going on. The last he had heard from her was when she signaled with the light that it was okay to discuss her presence with Suzy. The poltergeist did not know what he was thinking until he addressed his counterpart.

"M J . . . Is it possible that the ghost handed you over to someone else and moved on?"

"No, Michael, no. I'm still here."

This only added to the pressure on Pearly Ghost. She must find a way.

Michael was so pleased that Suzy liked the stick. Just as gratifying was that she appreciated his sense of humor. They were taking things slow and easy, but he was ready to take their bonding to another level. She was on her way over.

Light rain was moving in, and a walk was in doubt. It was too early to begin dinner, so the couple settled in the lounge. Michael took the lead.

"Suzy . . . Do you believe in fate?"

"I suppose that all depends upon what you mean by the term."

"Are guiding forces at work that open and close doors?"

Pearly Ghost was mesmerized. She momentarily forgot about her conundrum.

"Are you asking me if determinism sometimes trumps freedom?"

"Not necessarily. What about karma?"

"Oh, I for sure believe in karma. I have seen it at work many times, both for the good and the bad."

"How can you be sure that it was not just people reaping what they have sown, both good and bad?"

"Michael . . . Where is this going?"

Pearly Ghost was impressed with her new playmate. She was straightforward. Meanwhile, Michael was collecting his thoughts.

"I guess it's about how we got reintroduced. We had both been looking at our school yearbooks just before you called. What are the odds of that? And, you showed up in my life at such a critical time when I needed your support."

"Michael . . . Don't overthink it. Let's just be. The rain is letting up. Maybe we can get a walk in, after all."

There it was. Right there in front of her. Why had she not thought of it before? Suzy's hiking stick.

"Sister Pearl . . . Are you getting senile?"

Suzy was leaving hers with Michael's just inside the basement door. Before they could get downstairs, Pearly Ghost took it and put it in the front seat of the woman's car. The comb incidents had worked well.

Whoa! The mischief-maker reconsidered.

"What if Suzy thinks I'm telling her to take her stick and go away? Maybe the bathroom is better. That should get her attention."

This ruse didn't feel right either. Then, it hit her. But of course. She would pull the same prank that she once did on Michael.

When the pair descended the basement steps and put on walking shoes, one stick was missing.

"Suzy . . . Did you change your mind and take it home with you?"

"No. I left it right here."

The spirit could not hear what else was said, but Michael let Suzy use his stick, and he commandeered the one it replaced. After a lively walk with more rain on the way, they ducked back inside just ahead of a downpour.

"Look what I found."

Suzy's hiking stick was right back where she last left it.

Pearly Ghost was disappointed that nothing else was said implicating her.

The play-pretty

Mother Pearl overheard Michael telling Suzy that he was running a little late but was on his way. The road to her town was becoming more and more familiar. So were her movements and mannerisms.

Michael was also on a mission. Suzy had a honey-do list for her favorite handyman. This made him feel useful and appreciated.

Pearly Ghost thought about staying home, but after pulling off the stick ploy, she felt a new sense of exuberance. Michael suspected that she was along for the ride.

"Good work with the stick. Suzy thinks you have accepted her. I hope so. Now just remember . . . We are her guests. Make nice."

Mother Pearl wanted to smack Michael and tell him he sounded too much like a composite of Absolute Being and Mother Superior.

"Make nice . . . Huh. This is your mother you're talking to."

While the adults in the room were testing their boundaries, the spirit went snooping. Suzy's boudoir was a new fertile playground. Sister Pearl had faint recollections of her childhood when she coveted such baubles and beads.

One green hair clasp, in particular, fascinated her. For a fleeting cosmic moment, she imagined herself at a school dance with the clasp cradling her long dark blond hair as she sashayed. Caressing it, she then conjured up a word that was long ago lost. Play-pretty.

Pearly Ghost decided to take her new toy home with her. When Michael was out and about, she played with it. The next time Suzy came over, she went to the guest bathroom to see if she left the clasp there. Then, she quizzed Michael to see if he had found it.

"No, but I know a couple of places to look."

It was on neither vehicle's car seat.

Mother Pearl left the couple alone as they talked well into the night, and the bottle of wine was drained. When Suzy lamented about the drive home, Michael told her that the guest bedroom was made and ready.

Bleary-eyed, she took him up on it. When Suzy Q turned down the covers, the play-pretty was on her pillow.

The playdate

Thinking perhaps that they should cool their emotional jets, Suzy invited Michael over for a playdate. . . As in Scrabble. The first thing Pearly Ghost noticed when they went inside was Suzy wearing the green hair clasp.

"Good . . . The woman is working with me."

Neither competitor could remember the last time they played the word game. The other guest looked on as everything seemed to go the way of the hostess. Michael got stuck with letters that he could not use, and Suzy always seemed to draw just what she needed. The final score was a blowout.

After a break, Michael asked for a rematch. The second game was a replay of the first. Trying not to rub it in too much,

Suzy told him that he was such a good sport, and she ordered a pizza. The loser paid.

As they finished clearing the table, Michael requested one more chance to redeem himself.

"Fine with me. You must be a glutton for punishment."

Subtly, Michael drew tiles from those closest to Suzy in the box. Simultaneously, his fortunes reversed. Suzy congratulated him for salvaging his ego.

As he was backing out of the drive, Michael addressed his passenger.

"So . . . You were playing games with me tonight. You and Suzy double-teamed me until I beat you at your own game. No need to answer. I know it was you."

Playing house

"Hope you don't think I'm moving in, but I brought a few things to leave here when I stay the night."

Michael was pleased. He had thought about suggesting that, but he did not want to appear too forward.

"That end of the house is yours."

"What about the basement? I brought some walking shoes and socks."

"No problem."

Suzy arrived early on the first of two days off, and the couple was embarking on another first. They were going grocery shopping together. Pearly Ghost stayed behind.

The find of the day was pork loin on sale. Michael fired up the slow cooker. There was just enough time to roast the pork in barbecue sauce for it to be ready for dinner.

With a free afternoon, Michael suggested a walk in the city park. Mother Pearl went along this time. The couple set off on a path around a lake. Michael's right hand and Suzy's left kept bumping into each other. When she could stand it no longer, Pearly Ghost stepped in and lent a helping hand.

Neither spoke as they continued walking, holding hands for the first time since running to the vehicle in the rain following the memorial service. Up ahead, a park bench beckoned. Michael struggled with what to say next, afraid that anything might sound lame. Suzy preempted.

"Why did you never marry?"

Michael never saw that coming. Mother Pearl was all ears.

"I don't know. I suppose I just never found a woman who considered me worthy of her."

"Are you sure it's not the other way around? I think there's more to it than that."

Michael looked straight ahead avoiding eye contact, unaware that the other entity was looking right into his as he went on.

"I don't know if I came into the world this way, or if it is because of how I was raised, but intimacy is very important to me."

"And that is a reason why you were never in a committed relationship? Where else were you expecting to find intimacy?"

Michael was ready for the conversation to be over, but Suzy deserved an explanation. He turned and faced her.

"Females always talked a good game when it came to romance, and the next thing I knew, I had been dumped. I never found a woman who could sustain intimacy. I'd rather be alone than trapped in a passionless relationship."

"Are you saying that it is women, not men who can't make commitments? I thought it was the other way around."

"I'm not saying anything like that. Please know that I see things from my own experiences. Other people see the world through theirs."

Mother Pearl was beside herself.

"Oh, my precious son . . . You inherited so much of that from me."

Michael was ready to turn the tables.

"What about you? Have you always been single?"

"No, I haven't. I was married once and lived with another man for a couple of years."

When Michael remained silent, she turned and faced him.

"Is that a problem?"

"Of course not. But I would be less than honest if I did not admit that I'm glad neither worked out."

He turned pensive.

"I cannot imagine any man being worthy of you."

Suzy Q abruptly leaned in. They looked into each other's eyes. Breathing was shallow. Magically, lips brushed for the first time.

Michael never saw that coming, either.

No one could see Pearly Ghost in an angelic pose.

As Suzy gathered herself to stand, she sat back down. Her foot had been resting on an *almost* perfect heart-shaped rock.

Suzy helped in the kitchen as they put together side dishes to go with the barbecue.

Body parts kept bumping into each other. Promptly, they moved apart with one or the other apologizing for getting in the way.

"I'll bet you're as cranky as an old spinster librarian about keeping order in your kitchen."

"I'll have to admit, it's taking some getting used to having somebody I keep bouncing off of. But I'm so happy that you are learning your way around this part of the house."

"I'll try to put things where they belong, but just remember. If something goes astray, somebody else lives here, too."

"Now, don't go blaming things on her. She might not like it."

Mother Pearl was listening in. Michael was wrong.

As bedtime approached, Michael's psyche was flipping summersaults as both went to separate bathrooms to prepare. It was unspoken that neither was going straight to bed without saying goodnight.

Michael thought about going ahead and putting on his pajamas, but he feared that might be inappropriate. When Suzy came out, she was wearing a robe. He could not control his eyes, and she did not seem to mind.

Words stumbled coming out of the gate. Suzy took her right index finger and put it to Michael's lips. With her own, she quelled the tension.

"Shhh."

She then puckered them.

Pearly Ghost went into that pose again.

"That was some kind of good barbecue. Where did you learn to fix it like that?"

"From a recipe in the cookbook that came with the crockpot. It's cool enough to put in jars to freeze. We'll do that later, and you can take some home with you."

"You're a better cook than I am."

"You know what they say about necessity. I'll bet you could whip up a mean breakfast. You helped put up the groceries, so you know what's in the fridge."

"You're on, but you clean up my mess."

"I'll make the coffee."

Michael thought aloud as he took a bathroom break before waking up Mr. Coffee.

"M J . . . I'm not sure I got the best end of that deal."

After breaking their fast, the poltergeist was looking on. With four hands filling the freezer jars, two bodies were in close proximity, and two minds were feeling less awkward.

When the bottom of the barrel was scraped, Michael opened a utility drawer to retrieve a marker to record the date on the jars.

"I always keep it right here in the front."

He scrambled the other contents looking for it.

"I wonder if it ran out of ink the last time I used it, and I forgot to buy another one. Oh, well. I'll mark them later. How about a walk?"

After putting the crock aside to soak, Suzy went to the basement and took a seat to change her shoes.

"Would you look at that?"

Almost invisible against the backdrop of the black socks, the missing marker was straddling her footwear.

Part X: Shushed

A mother thing

Pearly Ghost was caught off guard when Ultimate Being reappeared suddenly. Neither was she prepared for the nature of the visit, but she should have been. The Divine was persistent that the time had come.

"What could possibly be left unfilled in your visitation?"

"I am so honored and grateful for the opportunity afforded me. I have not forgotten that glimpse of Glory. Crossing over for good will be so amazing and exciting. I can hardly wait."

"Do I detect a 'but' in there somewhere?"

"You're right. But I'm afraid Michael might need me soon?"

"How so? Things seem to be going well for him."

"It's a mother thing. You wouldn't understand."

It was not often that the Supreme was put on the defensive. Best to ignore that little dig. The Creator endured far worse insults from his creatures every day.

The ensuing pause was killing the transient spirit. What exactly was her Divine Superior mulling over? She braced herself.

"I'll let you stay a while longer, but I'm thinking seriously about setting a deadline."

Sister Pearl was fully aware that she might have crossed a cosmic line. Maybe an act of conciliation was in order.

"Deadline . . . I so love your sense of humor."

The bemused Divine Presence ended the appearance with no mention of a firm date.

Michael was cooking. Suzy Q was coming over later, and Mother Pearl wanted in on the action. She still preferred not to share her kitchen with anyone but her son. The ghost had little understanding of food, but utensils were another matter.

Michael muttered something under his breath about how hard it was to open packaged stuff. He reached for the scissors for an assist, but they were not in the tool caddy where he kept them.

"M J . . . Those are my kitchen scissors. They never leave this area. I have others that I use elsewhere. What could have possibly happened to them? Maybe Suzy misplaced them."

The real culprit looked on with amusement as the cook started searching the drawers and cabinets. With his cooking getting out of sync, the chef gave up and retrieved a pair from his office.

Suzy was running late, and Michael put everything on hold. Without mentioning her tardiness, she offered to set the table while he was putting the food out. Pearly Ghost was watching when Suzy opened the silverware drawer and came out with something that did not belong.

"Michael . . . What are the scissors doing in here? I thought you kept them on the counter."

His assumption about Suzy was wrong.

"You just got here, so I can't blame it on you. Maybe somebody else had something to do with it."

Pearly Ghost took a bow.

Mother Pearl was always looking on when Michael channeled his thoughts into his electronic journal. Of late, he was grappling with his feelings for Suzy. He mentioned how openness and transparency were woven into the fabric of his being, and that withholding his emotions was unnatural.

After dinner, the couple retired to the parlor for coffee and dessert.

"That was all so good. My compliments to the chef. You know what? I might just keep you around."

Things inside Michael were in a holding pattern. Suzy was rather certain where he was going when he turned and faced her. As before, she put her index finger to his lips.

"Shhh."

This was not a sleepover night. Suzy had undisclosed plans for the following day. Michael walked her to the car thinking this was the time to whisper something in her ear. She stopped him just in time.

"Shhh."

No passion was in Suzy's kiss, and she drove off into the night. Mother Pearl was by his side when he went back inside.

A hint of green

Michael never wearied of his private trails, but on occasion, he went walking elsewhere. On a bright sunny day, the city park was calling. He was not much into fast food, but he picked up a makeshift picnic. Strolling along the lake, he tried to ignore the pesky ducks begging for a handout.

Coming around a bend, he spotted *the* bench. Only, it was occupied.

"M J . . . I wish that person would move on."

As if on cue, the man's dog wanted to play ball again.

"You, lucky dog, you. You have somebody to play ball with. Bet you thought I was talking about the spaniel. Not so. I was thinking about this old mutt."

As Michael brought out the vittles, it was a bit breezy. He thought everything was secure until a napkin went flying. Before any chance of it getting very far away, it reversed course and landed at his feet.

"How did the wind change its direction so abruptly? Was it a whirlwind?"

Mother Pearl sighed.

After finishing his make-do lunch, Michael's emotions got all tangled up in the memories of the last time he sat in that same spot. This was *their* bench—The place where they first kissed.

As he got up to leave, he took a photo to email to Suzy. If he had looked closely before sending it, he might have noticed a hint of green in the blue sky background.

With time on his hands between rendezvouses with Suzy, Michael spent more of it in his shop. While working on something special for his lady friend, he let his mind go where it pleased.

"Michael Jonas . . . Wouldn't it be nice if Suzy went ahead and retired early? With no dependents or rent to pay, she could move in with us. We could manage just fine. Oh, what fun that would be?"

As he reloaded the sander, he added.

"But for now, I'm mired down in her shush."

Three days later, Michael went grocery shopping on the way to Suzy's. He showed up ready to start preparing supper soon after she got home. His lady friend had mentioned some other things that she needed help with while he was there. He put hamburgers on the grill while she went to take a bath.

"M J . . . I wonder if that door is locked. Don't even think about it. If you rattled the knob, you might get the shush knocked out of you."

After the condiments were back in the refrigerator and the dirty plates in the dishwasher, Suzy went over the work order. She was a good gofer as they made play out of work. Once the tools were back in his SUV, the couple settled on the sofa. Michael was in the mood for some cuddling when his overtures were interrupted.

"I need to go see a woman about a cat."

"And I need to see a man about a dog."

As they settled back down, the spell was broken. Michael excused himself a little earlier than usual under the guise that she must get up early the next morning and go to work.

When he drove into the garage and opened the door, he saw a bag on the passenger floorboard. Somebody sent him home with a leftover hamburger. That somebody also brought along a play-pretty.

Benched

Michael turned his attention back to the wood project. He had selected another cherry with blisters encircling the trunk. He squared one end and drilled out the other. The irregular growth made the piece resemble a decorative bottle where candle wax had flowed down. After it finished curing, the one-of-a-kind candle holder would be ready. The artisan was looking forward to showing off his handiwork.

Mother Pearl went back inside. Her son had purchased a new beard trimmer, and she was on her way to check it out. The power unit was separate from a little bag of accessories. Just right for her little bag of tricks.

When Michael noticed that his facial hair needed trimming, the tool bag was missing. Pearly Ghost watched with glee as he looked in places where she might have hidden it.

"He knows he did not misplace it. He understands it was me, but he will never find it."

Unable to locate the accessories, the clock was ticking. Suzy was coming over the next day, and he was more than a bit scruffy.

"M J . . . It didn't cost that much. Let's run into town and get another trimmer just like it. At least, we can interchange the parts."

After the buildup, Suzy called and canceled. She was not feeling well.

Michael was in a funk, and he went to the park. It was still a full week before he would see Suzy again. The disconsolate man wondered if she was married to her job. It felt like he was always playing second fiddle. Pearly Ghost knew this because he said so in his writings. She conjured up that expression from her youth.

The man was so much in need of a, or perhaps more specifically, some reality checks. He was having a hard time keeping his head and heart on the same page. Mother Pearl had read about that, too. With no one that he could see within earshot, he addressed his ever-present cohort.

"M J . . . Suzy is so much fun. Yet, when I want us to put our cards on the table, she shushes me. What's the deal?"

"What? No comment?"

He tried to put himself in her place. Deep down inside, Michael understood that Suzy was still making a living. She did not have the same freedom and flexibility that he did. Was there any possibility that she might quit her job so that they could be full-time playmates?

Pearly Ghost had heard it all before.

Then, the symbolism of where he was sitting rose and bit him in the butt.

"Michael Jonas . . . Have I been benched?"

Benefits

After almost three weeks, Suzy was finally coming his way. She was hesitant until Michael mentioned that he had a surprise for her. His old high school flame was pleased with the candle holder, and that made all of his efforts worthwhile.

"I tapered the top so that any regular-size candle will fit snuggly."

"Michael . . . You are so talented and thoughtful."

Sister Pearl said, "Amen," but no one heard her.

A damper of sorts was already on the evening. Suzy was expecting a business call that she must take.

"Michael . . . Are you ever going to get a cell phone?"

"Can't say that I would have enough use for one to justify the cost."

The call came right in the middle of dinner. Suzy went into the bathroom and closed the door, but that did not keep all parties out.

When the woman returned to the table, she said the call confirmed what she suspected. She must attend a called library board meeting the next morning and was not staying the night. Michael felt it best to stay quiet, or else he might say something that he would later regret. Suzy saved him by deflecting the conversation.

"That was a coworker on the phone. She and her man friend have an interesting relationship. They call it friends-with-benefits."

She looked at Michael for a reaction.

"Why would anyone be friends if there were no benefits? Isn't that what friends are for?"

Both females rolled their eyes.

Leaving Michael with the cleanup, Suzy needed to get on home and do some preparation for the meeting. He did not receive a hello hug, and he was denied kissing her goodbye. As the tail lights were going up the drive, he called out as though she could hear him.

"Wait. You forgot your . . ."

With that, Michael went to the drawer where he kept candles. A pretty green one stood out from the rest, and it fit just fine. He decided not to mention the stunning wood piece again. If Suzy wanted it, she would have to ask for it.

He then opened his e-journal and began writing. Other eyes followed along.

"M J . . . That was brilliant how you diverted the friends-with-benefits thing. Was that a come-on? Is this what Suzy Q wants from you?"

He hesitated and redirected.

"That woman has certainly been the beneficiary of some good benefits. I do all the cooking and most of the cleaning up afterward. She doesn't seem to mind at all that I pay for everything. And that's on top of my handyman services."

Michael paused and looked up before his fingers returned to the keyboard.

"Something else has been bothering me. I've never been invited to stay over at her house. And we don't go out together in her town. She shushed me when I mentioned visiting her at work."

Another reflective pause.

"Michael Jonas . . . Have the benefits gotten a little out of balance? Is Suzy Q just using you?"

He looked up and the candle had gone out.

"I thought I told you not to play with fire."

Mother Pearl was not miffed by the rebuke. It might take him a few minutes, but she hoped he would soon get the message she was sending.

On the road again

"My wonderful most special friend Michael, we need to talk."

"Your place or mine?"

"You are such a dear. Do you mind coming here?"

"Be there in less than an hour."

Fortunately, Michael could drive and think.

"What is this all about? The way she buttered me up, it must be something serious."

The other passenger was just as inquisitive. He arrived to open arms and a peck on the cheek.

"Can I get you anything?"

"No. I'm fine."

"Come. Let's sit."

This was Suzy's show, and Michael waited for her opening line.

"I'm sure you are aware that things have been happening with me. Thanks for not being nosey. I wanted to tell you all about it, but the ones involved were all sworn to secrecy."

He nodded for her to go on.

"I've been offered a Library Director position."

"Congratulations. I know this promotion is well-deserved."

"I knew you would say that, but there's more. It's at a large flagship library on the other side of the state."

He said nothing, but it was obvious that his feathers drooped.

"Michael . . . Don't be this way. Talk to me."

"I hope karma gets you everything you deserve. What more is there for me to say?"

"I don't want to lose you."

"I'm proud both of and for you. I honestly am. But I have been thinking lately about how nice it would be if you took early retirement so that we could ride off into the sunset together."

"Michael . . . You don't know how much I'd love that. Just please understand how important this is to me. I've been picked over for promotions when less-qualified men got the job. Then, I was snubbed by minority picks. I did not get a graduate degree in library science to abandon my unfulfilled goals and ambitions."

Michael did not have an answer for that. Suzy continued.

"You had your own business. You ran it well so that you could spin off early. I admire you so much for that. But the realization of my dream is finally happening. I can't walk away from it just now."

She lowered her head before continuing.

"I could never ask you to give up your place and move with me."

"Thanks for understanding that."

"I'll come by when I have a chance and pick up my things."

"Just let me know when so I can be there."

"I thought you were going to say so you would *not* be there."

Michael turned and headed to his vehicle. Just beyond the outskirts of the town, he spoke aloud.

"M J . . . I was beginning to know this road like the back of my hand. Now, I might never come this way again."

Pearly Ghost's ears perked up when the phone rang.

"Michael . . . Could I ask just one more favor? I'm overwhelmed getting ready for this move. Would you please gather up my things and bring them to me? It shouldn't be that hard to figure out what's not yours. Don't want another woman to stumble upon my stuff."

"I don't want them in my house, but it has nothing to do with another woman."

"Please don't be bitter. If it's too much trouble, just toss everything."

"I'll get them to you."

On the way, the driver made an onboard correction.

"M J . . . I *am* going down this road one more time."

Michael almost forgot the hiking stick and walking shoes. Nothing was said about the ornate candle holder. Neither was there mention of anything that Pearly Ghost might be hoarding. The couple tiptoed all around saying goodbye. One more time, he just turned and walked away.

Michael was unmotivated for the next few days. Standing beside the little waterfall one evening as the light was fading, it was not a big stretch to put things in perspective.

"Old boy . . . No wonder you're so down in the dumps. You've been dumped. Fate dealt you a tricky hand, and it had a joker in it."

When he came inside from the walk, flickering candlelight was making shadows on the walls. A wraith hovered nearby. Michael let the candle burn.

Part XI: Heaven's gate

Beep . . . Beep . . . Beep

Michael was in a deep sleep just before daybreak when back to back to back beeps woke him up.

"M J . . . Does a smoke alarm have a dead battery?"

Something was not right about that. This chirping was different. He got up, turned on a light, and went in the direction of the sounds. They stopped.

Pearly Ghost was looking around for a way to cheer Michael up and lift his spirits. This was the best tactic that she could come up with.

Awake now, he started coffee. The triple beeps happened again. It seemed as though they were coming from the lounge area. Michael positioned himself beneath the smoke detector and waited. Nothing happened.

The bizarre beeps chimed in still another time. It sounded like they were in the kitchen. He went and stood underneath the detector in that room. Nothing happened.

The sounds then began moving from room to room with Michael chasing them. His rational mind was testing the limits of its circuit breakers. He could not identify anything responsible for the noises. They did not seem to be emitting from any single electronic device.

Then, they stopped.

As Michael prepared breakfast, he continued processing.

"Is something defective, and is this like a check engine light coming on?"

As he stacked the dirty dishes in the sink, another light came on.

"Does this have anything to do with you?"

A single beep sent back to back to back to back chills running up and down Michael's spine.

Honk . . . Honk . . . Honk

Michael had avoided the city park long enough. He walked at a hefty gait, and other than bypassing *the* bench, nothing else was on his mind.

The green space was pet-friendly, and numerous owners were walking their dogs. The man meandering observed people stopping and chatting with the animals the center of attention.

"M J . . . Maybe you should get a dog. Folks might stop and talk to you."

His musing was interrupted as a flock of geese came from over the horizon honking at full throttle. Michael watched as they circled the large lake and located a landing spot. Mother Pearl wondered what her son was thinking, but she must wait until they got back home to find out.

He did not go immediately to the computer, and the spirit grew restless. She had observed his face in cogitation mode and knew something was up. Eventually, he took a seat and began compiling.

"I don't need a dog. Oh, sure, a pet could provide lots of company. I think those geese were trying to tell me something else. Maybe I should start tooting my own horn. Yeah, right. Who would give a rat's toenail regarding my opinions about anything?"

He shuffled his shoulders to relax them.

"I think the geese were suggesting that it is time for me to do some migrating of my own. I don't need to fritter my life away waiting for a playmate. I *am* taking exception to one possible inference, though. Just not interested in large group travel."

Before he closed the computer, Pearly Ghost saw bedevilment in his eyes.

"Michael Jonas . . . In the game of love, you're in the late innings, and your score is one big fat goose egg."

Yes . . . Yes . . . Yes

"M J . . . What would it be like to fly like a goose? My feet have never been off the ground."

His birthday was coming up soon, and Michael decided to treat himself. After looking at various options, he narrowed it down to three possibilities—Barnstorming in an open-cockpit single-engine plane, parasailing, or taking a ride in a hot air balloon. Pearly Ghost heard him as he spoke aloud.

"I do not want to be on the evening news."

When he called and reserved a spot for a late afternoon hot air balloon ride on his birthday eve, Mother Pearl was delighted.

"Yes . . . Yes . . . Yes."

Pearly Ghost decided to go along. The flight was standing room only, but she didn't take up any space. The passengers were all congenial and listened as the pilot filled them in on what to expect. The airship was dependent on wind currents, but they were assured that someone on the ground would be chasing them.

As the tethering was released, the gas jets fired, and the craft began its ascent. While everyone else was looking down as they went up, Mother Pearl kept an eye on her son. She was concerned about him after Suzy moved away.

The balloon drifted quietly except for the periodic bursts to replenish the uplifting heat. Reverence settled in as the sun was setting. It was almost dark when the basket bounced a time or two on a ball field before coming to a stop.

The ghost could only imagine what Michael thought of the experience. From his persona, he had enjoyed it. She knew how she felt.

117

"Sister Pearl . . . When you set out to lift his spirits, you simply outdid yourself."

When Michael opened his computer the next morning, he was greeted again by bold green letters.

No . . . No . . . No

Pearly Ghost confiscated a spare remote garage door opener and had a new toy to add to her collection. When Michael came down the drive and activated the mechanism, she pushed the button on hers. This reversed the door's direction, and it was down when the vehicle circled to enter. When the puzzled driver hit the switch again, it went back up.

As he was leaving one day, she pulled the same prank. The noise stopped, and Michael put the SUV in reverse not realizing that the door had come back down.

"No . . . No . . . No."

Just in the nick of time, she started it opening again. Michael hit the brakes when he heard the commotion.

"Whew! That could have put a dent in my wallet."

While in town, he discussed the malfunction with a man at the hardware store. The ghost was listening when the counter clerk made a suggestion.

"Maybe it has a hitch in its get-a-long—Like a burr or rough spot that triggers the safety mechanism. Spray this lubricant on all moving parts."

Mother Pearl watched as Michael followed the man's directions. He then raised and lowered it two or three times for the grease to get in all the cracks and crevices.

"M J . . . It seems to be working fine."

After no more glitches, Michael decided that the remedy had worked. Pearly Ghost realized that she must be more careful when playing with the gadget.

As her clutch grew, Pearly Ghost was always on the lookout for a better hiding place to keep her playthings. She had moved her keepsakes from under the cushion of the guest bedroom chair, to the floor beneath the sofa, behind the washing machine, to under the tapestries inside the dresser drawer.

One night, she took her toys to the couch in the lounge and spread them. The ghost proudly looked over her stash. Her prized possession was still the green hair clasp. Other trinkets included lip gloss, a bar of soap, a toothbrush, the cinnamon tin, three rubber bands, a pencil, a washcloth, a belt, a screwdriver and a pair of pliers from the shop, the beard trimmer accessories, a large butcher knife from a kitchen drawer, a spare house key, some money, and the corkscrew, which Michael had not missed. Most wine he brought home came with screw caps.

Suddenly, a light came on in the bedroom.

"No . . . No . . . No."

The spirit reached for and activated the garage door opener. Hastily, she shuffled her playthings out of sight under the sofa.

When Michael went to check, the garage door was back down, but the light was still on. Yet, a third light came on, this one in his head.

"I love you, too."

"Yes . . . Yes . . . Yes."

There . . . He said it again.

Ring . . . Ring . . . Ring

The ocean was calling Michael, and Mother Pearl was listening in. The phone did not ring often, but when it did, nosey Pearly Ghost positioned herself to find out what was going on. If

Michael held the receiver too close to his ear, she could hear only one side of the conversation. He sometimes picked up on her vibes and put it on speaker.

This call was from an insurance agent from back when the now self-unemployed man got up and went to work. The former associate owned a condo with a view of the ocean. The facility was used a couple of times for working vacations.

Michael had declined offers for personal use while the employee worked for him. It was different now.

The unexpected call with an invitation to visit the beachfront property was enticing. To sweeten the pot, the owner mentioned that early fall was the best time to go. Students were back in school, and most snowbirds had not yet arrived. If he wished, the unit was his for a week.

Pearly Ghost's eyes were watching when he journaled before the trip. She learned that it was not too far out of the way to go through the town where Suzy lived.

The ghost could not remember seeing the sea, or she might have let Michael go alone. She was a bit perturbed when he packed the candle holder. On the way down, Mother Pearl listened as her son had a conversation with himself.

"Michael Jonas . . . You sure acted like a silly schoolboy with that woman. Your feelings blinded you to Suzy's agenda. She was still earning her credentials and paying her dues while you were in a much different place. You cannot fault her for doing what was in her best interest."

The driver switched off the radio and continued talking to himself.

"Suzy's situation is not that different from most women of my generation. Maybe I should marry a wealthy widow and see what it feels like to be a rich bastard. Nope. Some people already treat me like I'm one, and I really have no desire to be rich."

Mother Pearl was horrified by his word choice. She still did not know if they were going to make the detour until Michael spoke again well on down the road.

"M J . . . That was the exit. We missed it. Let's go to the beach."

After he checked in and unpacked, they did just that. A few parents were keeping watch over their preschoolers. Mother Pearl got all choked up thinking about playing in the sand with her little boy.

Before bedtime, she wanted to know what Michael was keyboarding. He was writing a poem entitled, "The Sound of the Sea in the Moonlight."

A steady breeze was blowing the following morning. Pearly Ghost spied several large birds just hanging out suspended in midair facing the currents.

"I can do that."

After lunch, the wind settled some. The spirit watched as a little boy and his dad were trying to fly a kite. Gusts lifted it airborne but then dropped it with a thud. The lad was getting more and more agitated.

On the next try, the kite gained altitude, and the string remained taunt as it climbed higher and higher. Sister Pearl spoke to herself.

"Wow! What a nice view from up here. I could get used to flying."

Mother Pearl was preoccupied with watching the full moon rise over the ocean. The only other light in the condo was from the candle. She did not notice that Michael had opened his computer. Just in time, she got a glimpse of what he was scribing. It was entitled, "Ebb and Flow."

The writer theorized that life is like the ebb and flow with its ups and downs. The onlooker got that. Then, he postulated that some people get stuck in the ebb and others mired in the flow. She had no idea what he was talking about.

Pearly Ghost got to use her kite-flying skills three more times. On the last night, Michael wrote something before packing his computer. It was entitled, "Mothers." She did know something about that.

Mother Pearl watched with interest as her son described the ocean as being like our primordial mother. He expressed how he felt when walking barefoot with the waves lapping at his feet. And he vowed not to stay away from reconnecting with this manifestation of Mother Earth for very long.

Michael grew still before closing.

"The sea is like our primal birthplace. A child grows in its mother's watery womb. Did we get something wrong? Shouldn't we call our planet, Mother Water?"

For what it was worth, his only reader and critic agreed with him completely.

Knock . . . Knock . . . Knock

The battery in the driveway monitor sending component had been dead for a couple of weeks, and Michael kept forgetting to pick up a replacement. One of Mother Pearl's playthings was temporarily disabled.

The unit approaching the front stoop was working fine. The day was chilly, and the main door was closed. The device got both residents' attention when it shattered the solitude. This was followed by a brusque repetitive clank.

"Knock . . . Knock . . . Knock."

As Michael went to see who the visitor was, he smiled remembering how his then unbeknownst ghost made him aware that the storm door deadbolt was not functioning properly. He had to unlock both to let the visitor in, but security was not an issue.

It took a moment for Pearly Ghost to recognize Michael's custodial father. The man began explaining how he was on his way back home after calling on some of his old clients.

"I decided that while I'm still able, I need to get out more."

It occurred to Michael that he could not see his parents without an appointment, but they could drop in on him unannounced. He made a conscious effort not to let that sour his disposition.

"I'm glad to know that you're doing well. Can I get you anything?"

"First, I need to go see a man about a dog."

Mother Pearl laughed so hysterically that her seamless garb almost wasn't.

The father and son soon settled in the parlor sipping cups of decaf and munching on black walnut brownies that had come out of the oven that morning. Michael was trying to come up with some fodder for the small talk mill, but his apprehension was unnecessary.

The man seemed more relaxed than Michael could remember. Was this just a social call? Somebody else was also listening in.

"Son . . . When you get my age, you spend a lot of time thinking about what if. What would you do differently if you had it to do all over again?"

Michael could not remember the last time his father called him "son." As a kid, that meant he was in trouble.

"Take me and your mother. I always thought I would go first."

The aging man dropped his head.

"I worked so hard to make sure that she was provided for."

Michael did not know what to say.

"Your mother kept begging me to retire. She wanted to travel and do all the things we had postponed when life got in the way. But I could just never see my way free and clear. As you know, by the time I got around to turning in my notice, her brain was already beginning to fail."

Michael was not the man's therapist, and he did not know how to respond. It seemed enough at the moment that he was listening. The subject shifted.

"I'm also troubled by how I was never able to tell my family members how much I loved them. With your mother, it was unnecessary. She knew."

"You two were very close."

"Michael . . . I came out of my way to come by here and tell you something before it's too late."

Pearly Ghost let out a gasp and was afraid someone might have heard her.

The man hesitated before going on.

"I want you to know how proud I am of you for getting out of the rat race when you did. Granted, you didn't have as many stumps to plow around as most folks do. I admire you so much for not being caught up in materialism."

"I'm low-maintenance. It does not take much for me to get by."

"Son . . . It's more than that. You owned your business, but it never owned you."

He paused again.

"I wish so much that I could have been more like you."

Tears welled in Michael's eyes.

"Thank you, Dad. I love you, too."

Mother Pearl could breathe a little easier again.

If Michael had known ahead of time that his father was coming, he might have remembered to ask him about the boxes in the basement. He did not think of them until the next day. Two days later, the phone rang. His dad had died of a massive heart attack.

"Michael Jonas . . . When that man came up on my front porch, he was already knocking on Heaven's gate."

Part XII: The Pearly Gate

Parlor visitations

Pearly Ghost was uncomfortable in the funeral parlor. How could she be sure that the dead man's spirit had crossed directly over? She moved from room to room and felt all kinds of vibes but nothing that was tied to Michael's adoptive father.

Mother Pearl knew her son was not looking forward to the scheduled visitation. He had written about how isolated he felt when his mother died. She was pleased when the mortician placed him at the head of the receiving line.

It might have seemed like a strange setting for another kind of visitation, but in the realm of the supernatural, everything is extraordinary. Above the din coming from the viewing room, Absolute Being appeared to the hovering spirit. Telepathic communications were undetectable to anyone below.

"I sensed your concern about the man's spirit. Let me assure you that it went right on into the light."

"That's a relief."

"Now that both of Michael's custodial parents have crossed on over, it is time for you to come with me."

"Oh, please. Not just now. Michael will need his mother as he charts the course for the rest of his life."

"Your son has some serious reckoning ahead. There is a considerable risk of you becoming an obstacle."

"Oh, I promise not to do that. Please let me stay and help him get through this."

Ultimate Being relented with the stipulation that if things went awry, the decision would be reversed on short notice.

Michael was not sure what he was feeling after it was all over. Mother Pearl could not read his thoughts on the way home. He did not journal for a couple of days. In the meantime, she kept contemplating something. What did her Superior mean by serious reckoning?

The color of money

When Michael's electric toothbrush would not come with a full charge, he went to the file where he kept warranties.

"M J . . . It probably expired last month."

He was wrong. It was two months. Mother Pearl was disappointed that he did not think of another explanation.

While the file box was open, Michael noticed the corner of something that did not belong. His fingers pulled out a $20 bill.

"Michael Jonas . . . How did that get there?"

Not nearly as meticulous as his parents were about keeping records, he saved receipts for a year and then recycled them unless a warranty was involved.

"There is no way on God's green earth that I put that piece of paper money in that file box. But what does it mean?"

Pearly Ghost was pleased when Michael decided to take himself out to lunch. He knew the bill was likely lifted from his wallet, but he treated it like an unanticipated gift.

"Who says there is no such thing as a free lunch?"

While chowing down, the spirit of his birth mother was hoping that he had made a connection. Maybe looking into his receipts would remind him of the boxes in the basement.

Over the next several days, he glanced at them.

"Michael Jonas . . . What's the hurry?"

After using a regular toothbrush for several days, without thinking, he reached for the electric one. It was working fine.

The family tree

Michael was out walking when he came upon a strange phenomenon. A pile of twigs was in the middle of the path. The small sticks were cut neatly into short pieces from green branches and placed in a circle.

"M J . . . No animal could have done anything like that, and so far as I know, no trespassers have been on my property. Anyway, this does not appear to be human activity. But what does it mean?"

Mystified, he chalked it up to another enigmatic incident. Three days later, he experienced an encore performance on another section of the trail. The first collection was made from hardwoods. The new twigs were all cut from evergreen cedar.

It was all very clear to Mother Pearl. She must trust Michael's subconscious to connect the dots to his branch on the family tree.

Michael was struggling with his sentiments, and trying to inscribe them was not very helpful. His father's death had him thinking about his destiny. So many blank pages were in the ledger of his life, and he could find no way to retro fill them.

Not sure where it came from, Michael's thoughts went to the day he was born. He remembered asking his mother about it, and her answer was vague.

"Michael Jonas . . . I wonder what else happened on that monumental day."

He surfed the web and found a few world events, but this did not satisfy him. Mother Pearl was intrigued when he wrote in his journal that he was going to see if he could find old copies of his hometown newspaper.

The receptionist was not very optimistic and called for help. Another newspaper person came to the desk and said for him to follow her. Soon, they were in the catacombs of the publishing company.

"We've been working to digitalize all of our old copies, but we have not gotten back that far."

"Are you telling me that I'm old?"

She ignored the question.

"All we ask is that you remove only one edition at a time and put it back before taking another one."

Michael found the year and then the month. Soon, the newspaper published on the day of his birth was spread on a worktable before him.

The front page headline was about a farmer whose cow had triplets. Advertisements caught his eye next.

"Things were sure cheap back then."

A weekly hospital report of babies born was near the middle. His name was not on it.

"Guess I missed the deadline."

Mother Pearl chuckled at his word choice. He then turned to the obituaries.

"M J . . . Some people are born and others die on the same day. At least these folks and three baby calves made the news."

The spirit was pleased that Michael pulled no other editions. While in town, he went to the cemetery. She could not make out what he was thinking while standing at the graves of his custodial parents.

For the record

As Michael came into the basement, he vowed to dispose of the boxes the next day. Not sure why he was putting it off, he imagined a quick check and then hauling the old records off to be recycled. That night with Mother Pearl looking on, he wrote about his hesitancy.

"It's like I'm ripping up my roots. These records are the last tangible vestige connecting me to my early life."

True to himself, after breakfast, Michael went down the steps. When he opened the first box, his plan went immediately into revision. It contained several years of tax records. Anything with confidential information would have to be shredded. The task was back on hold.

Mother Pearl was pleased that her son was close to moving on from all that he had been through. She was trying to find a way to light a fire under him, but he was galloping along at his slow gait. She went into her angel pose when he brought a shredder home.

"M J . . . This is a much bigger project than I imagined. We must go through everything to make sure there is no personal information. This cheap shredder sure is slow."

After working an hour or so for three mornings, the first box was ready for disposal. The oldest son needed a break before tackling the other one.

Michael had not washed the sheets on the guest bed since Suzy last slept on them. Neither had he cleaned the bathroom. When he kneeled to wash out the tub, a torrent of water doused him from the shower head.

The diverter from tub to shower was designed to release when the water was turned off. Michael tried to make it hang again and couldn't.

"Somebody must think I need a bath."

After finishing the grunt work, he went to his bathroom and did just that. Groceries were running low. He brewed some tea in his travel mug to sip on the way to town.

After the pantry, freezer, and refrigerator were restocked, he rinsed the stainless steel mug and placed it in the drainer. When he went to put it back in the cabinet, the lid was missing.

"M J . . . I remember distinctly washing them both."

He did the usual of checking the vehicle and looking all around the kitchen. He put the mug in the cabinet until its misplaced part showed back up.

Michael had forgotten about the lid until he decided to take some tea with him while tackling the other cardboard box. The lid was sitting atop the mug as though it had not been off wandering.

A treasure trove

Michael was in for a big surprise when he opened the remaining box. It contained his parents' financial record books over several decades. They started the year the couple got married.

He was impressed with how meticulous the entries were. Michael imagined hard times when the newlyweds had to account for every nickel. The oldest son grabbed three or four and took them upstairs.

"What a treasure trove. And just think. It has been in my basement all this time."

To say that Michael was mesmerized would be an understatement. Mother Pearl was looking over his shoulder. Seeing how his parents allocated meager resources was such an important part of their history. And his, too. The shredder took a rest.

"M J . . . If I were an author, I could write a book about this."

The last ledger he brought up was from the year before he was born. Enough for that day.

As he sat at the computer, Michael struggled to find the right words. He was overwhelmed by how much of people's history dies with them. What might become of his journaling? Would it just give up the ghost when his computer crashed?

Michael was not looking for anything in particular when he perused the accountings of his birth year. His father had a steady job and deposited his check regularly. At the end of some months, there was very little to carry over.

His excitement built as he turned the pages. The firstborn found an entry for a baby bed. It was the same one handed down to his little brother and sister.

"Would you look at that? They went to a movie on the day before I was born."

Michael was seeing snippets of his living history. Ready to close the book on his birth year, something stopped him. He went back over the figures carefully. There was no record of any payments to a doctor or a hospital.

"Michael Jonas . . . Were you a charity case?"

Since Michael knew what was in the box, there was no hurry to finish going through it. Mother Pearl watched as he wrote into his chronicles.

"I feel like a kid peering through the keyhole of my parent's bedroom door. Then again, there must not be anything secretive in these records. Else, they would not have been left in my custody."

That last word did not get past Pearly Ghost. What happened the following day proved him wrong. When he pulled out the next record book, a corner of something was sticking out from beneath the rest. Out came an envelope marked "Confidential."

Emotions overcame Michael that he could not explain. His vocabulary failed when he tried to write about it. Mother Pearl knew they were on sacred turf.

He did not put this unexpected find back in the box but rather took it upstairs. Michael vacillated between shredding it unopened and taking a look inside. It was likely something that the statute of limitations had run out on years ago, and it just never got tossed.

He tossed and turned trying to decide what to do. All of his intuitions kept blinking red. Pearly Ghost stood by anxiously.

The bolt from the blue

Michael had dillydallied long enough. He just went ahead and sliced open the yellowed envelope and removed the contents. For the next few moments, he had to steady himself.

Michael held in his hand adoption papers with his name on them. He put them aside and bleary-eyed, he went outside.

Mother Pearl was by his side unsure of what he was thinking. He had not gotten to the place where other names were on the form. Everything about her future and his was very much on the line.

She left him and went back to the house to make sure. The apparition looked inside the envelope. There it was in black and white. Pearl White was listed as the child's birth mother.

Her memories of that time were blurred, but she had a vague recollection of her parents signing over their grandparental rights. That page was missing. All Michael had to go on was her earthly name.

Michael's emotional state was fragile as he talked to birds stationed all along the trail. Some things finally made sense, but this opened up another world of compelling unknowns. It cut to the very core of his being and identity. Mother Pearl caught back up with her son just in time to hear him ask a question aloud.

"Michael Jonas . . . Who the devil do you think you are?"

Over the next few hours, the floundering man rummaged for a foothold. He had been deceived his entire life. Michael simply could not wrap his mind around plausible circumstances for him being handed off and not being told. Mother Pearl was attentive when he spoke aloud.

"What about my siblings? Were they adopted, too?"

For the first time in his life, the oldest son considered hand-me-down resemblances. He could see common features in the other family members, but he looked like none of them. Why had he never noticed that before?

"Were my parents unable to have a baby? Did they adopt me and then have two of their own? That sort of thing happens. I am six years older than the next one in line."

Michael eventually picked up the confidential forms again. For the first time, he saw the name of his birth mother—Pearl White. The father was listed as "Unnamed."

Pearly Ghost swooned. Her son knew his mother's name. Oh, how the ghost yearned to oust herself.

Michael also read that the birth records were permanently sealed unless the adoptive parents decided to tell their son. It did not come to him as some kind of vision. Rather it evolved slowly in his mind.

"M J . . . I think my father wanted me to know. There was no slouching in the way he took care of his business. It's hard for me to imagine that this was a careless blunder. That man must have known what he was doing when he left the boxes with me. Just think. That sealed envelope was right there in my basement all the while."

Something else took shape in his thoughts.

"Do you suppose telling me about this was the real reason for his visit just before he died? And he just couldn't bring himself to go through with it?"

Dead ends

Michael wanted to know who his birth parents were. And yet, he didn't.

"M J . . . Why are you fretting so? You don't have a ghost of a chance tracking them down."

Mother Pearl sighed and watched nervously as he typed her name into a search engine browser. Several links popped up regarding the Sister with the same name who died in a mass shooting saving her mother.

"I remember seeing that on the news. What a story, but that's a dead end. She was a nun, for Christ's sake."

He followed links to the obituaries of two Pearl Whites. One was too old, and the other was not old enough.

"White was most likely her maiden name. Chances are she married, and there is no way of finding her."

Pearly Ghost was aware that he got only one out of three right.

With nothing but time on his hands, he typed in Pearl W. Several references came up on the screen, but none with White.

Mother Pearl watched intently as he journaled that evening.

"I want to know, and yet, I don't. If my birth mother wanted me in her life, why did she not find me?"

"Oh, my precious son. You are so dead wrong."

Then he added.

"But if the records were sealed, maybe she had no way."

Michael had a decision to make. Should he discuss this startling revelation with his brother and sister?

"Michael Jonas . . . I think not. Let their lives and memories be unaffected. You were treated as an equal when the estate was settled. Why rock the boat?"

Pearly Ghost knew it was going to happen. Just not when. When was sooner than later. Absolute Being was very much aware of what was going on. She preempted.

"Okay . . . He knows he was adopted, but I had nothing to do with it. I could have put the confidential forms in his path, but I didn't. Besides that, he has already checked me off the list."

"I cannot argue with any of that. But how long do you think it will take his inquisitive mind to connect the dots between his resident spirit and his birth mother?"

"What would be so bad if he did?"

"You might have a point there."

Pleased with another deferment after the close call, Pearly Ghost settled back in.

In the blink of an eye

Michael could not get the news story off his mind. Even though he had ruled out the legendary Sister, that she shared the same name as his mother intrigued him.

The convent was on the other side of the big city. Michael got up early one morning and set off for an adventure. His passenger was not so sure about this.

Two hours later, he found a parking spot and walked around to the main entrance. Just as the reporting had indicated, "The Pearly Gate" was inscribed on the massive door.

The knob rattled and two residents came out, at first oblivious to a visitor. One retraced her steps.

"Can we help you?"

"I was just passing through and couldn't resist the temptation to come by and see this door. May I take a photo of it?"

"Of course. We once had lots of visitors, but not that many now. Would you like a tour?"

"I don't know why not."

"Mother Superior will want to meet you first."

After an exchange of pleasantries, she asked if he could stay for lunch.

"I don't want to be an imposition."

"No trouble at all. I'll catch up with you later."

Mother Superior had lost a step, but she thought she heard him right. Just in case.

"What did you say your name is?"

Pearly Ghost was tripping all over herself. She almost wished she hadn't come. At every venue, shadowy memories resurfaced. Not all were good. She was ready for this visit to be over.

The head of the convent locked the door, located the hidden key, and opened the secured cabinet. She thought her memory was right, and it was. This was trouble. She began rehearsing how she might handle it. With both of Michael's parents deceased, this file was permanently sealed.

On the way to the gardens and greenhouse, Michael noticed some standing stones in a grove.

"Is Sister Pearl buried there?"

"Yes. Would you like to visit her grave?"

"I think I would."

After three paces in that direction, Michael stopped and picked up something. Only the spirit knew that Michael was standing at his mother's grave. All present watched as he placed a beautiful white heart rock on Sister Pearl's earthly resting place.

Pearly Ghost was dumbstruck.

The guides showed off their handiwork in the gift shop.

"We strand these."

The labeling identified them as Sister Pearl beads.

"Is that her picture?"

"Yes. It was taken not long before she passed away."

Pearly Ghost was petrified, frozen in a time warp. Michael was standing there looking at a photograph of his mother.

Mother-of-pearl jewelry boxes were alongside the beads.

"We order the shells, fashion them, attach them to the outsides, and sell them in memory of Sister Pearl."

Michael was impressed with the handiwork. Just as he said he would like to purchase one, Mother Superior walked up.

"My gift to you."

"Then, let me contribute to your treasury."

"You can do that when we get to the chapel. Follow me."

Upon entering, Michael turned to the left and lit a candle. Another started burning beside it. After reaching into his wallet, the residents and visitors started down the aisle. Michael turned in at a pew and knelt. Others joined him on the other side. The invisible guest worshiped at the altar.

Michael mentioned how good the food was.

"We grow much of it on the abbey grounds."

Pearly Ghost wanted this to be over, but Michael seemed in no hurry.

"What was Sister Pearl like?"

Mother Superior frowned, but no one at the table noticed. This was nothing out of the ordinary for her. Both Sisters jumped in at the same time. One yielded.

"She was witty. If others were having a bad day, she seemed to know just what to do or say to brighten the mood and lift their spirits."

The other nun stepped in.

"And mischievous. She loved pulling her little pranks."

Pearly Ghost was doing backflips as her old peers continued.

"Behind her back, we called her 'Sista Pranksta.' She was an honorary Tomfoolery gangsta member."

Sister Pearl was beside herself.

"Behind my back, my foot. And you did not get away with other stuff, either, like you thought you did."

The first speaker grew serious.

"There were times when Sister Pearl seemed to go somewhere deep into herself. We all knew just to let her be."

Michael had a question.

"Isn't meditation a customary part of your spiritual life?"

"Yes. But it went beyond that. She was in a space where no one else was allowed."

The spiritual entity in the room grew sad.

Mother Superior's stern expression had not dissolved when Michael turned to her.

"How do you remember Sister Pearl?"

The muscles in her face relaxed a bit.

"I would say that she was reverently irreverent."

That tickled Pearly Ghost's ethereal funny bone.

After scrumptious strawberry cobbler and coffee, Michael made eye contact with all around the table.

"I have a question that might sound a little weird."

All eyes shifted to him.

"After Sister Pearl's tragic death, did you ever feel her spirit around here?"

All eyes turned to the one at the head of the table.

"Those of us who have open minds about the spirit world sort of expected that we would. But nothing ever happened that we associated with her."

Abruptly, the lights went out. With few windows, the big hall was almost dark. And then, they came back on. Michael felt a chill.

After lunch and some goody bags to take with him, he told his friendly hostesses goodbye. Mother Superior breathed a big sigh of relief, but she wondered if he would be back.

When the man and his silent partner got home, he did not go directly inside. The moon was coming up over the trees, and he watched the circle of light grow brighter.

As he came back into the garage, the door began closing before he touched the wall mount. Once inside, Michael stood motionless in the shadows. Time stood still.

"*Mother?*"

In the blink of an eye, flickering candlelight dispelled the darkness.

Afterglow

Over the next several years, Michael grew old and not always gracefully. Pearly Ghost reminded him all along that his *mother* was still right there with him. The Creator checked on them now and then.

On a warm summer night, the window was open, fireflies were flickering, tree frogs were serenading, gentle breezes rustled the leaves, and the wind chimes were playing a harmonious melody. With Absolute Being as their guide, Michael Jonas and Pearly Ghost crossed over into the Light of Glory—Together.

About the author

Larry G. Johnson is a prolific writer of both fiction and nonfiction. Drawing from personal experiences and using his vivid storytelling imagination, he is the author of a five-volume family saga that spanned more than a century.

The War Baby

Miss Bizzy Belle

God's Frozen Chosen

Robin's Song

Walt's Mountain

Johnson has also produced a photo journal, *Frozen in Time*, a compilation of amazing photographs with compelling stories to go with them.

In *A Blue Plate Special at the Blue Goose Café*, the writer followed the advice that he has given to countless when he chronicled numerous amusing coming-of-age character-building episodes of his life.

Little Orphan Andy is an epic tale centered on a true story about a rescued orphan fawn. This heart-warming volume is a deer little children's book for the child in all of us.

The writer took his story-telling skills in a very different direction in, *She Wore Green*. This narrative draws from his experiences with a residential ghost. One day he had a *novel* idea. Why not compose a tale through the eyes of a ghost? As the author embarked on the project, he got a clear and unmistakable go-ahead signal from his poltergeist. Many of these episodes are straight from his journaling. He suspects the notion to write this book was not an original thought.

Over a couple of decades, the author spent considerable time in Alaska. He is privileged to reside in a retreat/sanctuary down on Walter Pond in Northwest Georgia.

lgj@mindspring.com